IMPUNITY

FAITH OSE EBHODAGHE

ISBN: 978-978-559-349-5

Book Cover and interior formatting by @thebookjedi_ (Instagram)

Published by Jali Books, an Imprint of Madda Book Media

A child who is not embraced by the village will burn it down to feel its warmth. When the flames die, and a new village emerges, that child will be crowned a hero when he becomes a man.

To my mother and sister, for their unwavering support.

To my extended family, for the chaos and love that shaped me.

To my lovely husband for being present when I couldn't be.

PREFACE

Corruption does not begin in the heart of elders—it is nurtured in classrooms, whispered in school hallways, and justified in the homes of ordinary people. It is a seed sown early, watered by impunity, and harvested by those who rise to power with no regard for justice.

Impunity is not just a story; it is a reflection of the reality we live in. It explores the origins of corruption, beginning in secondary school, where young minds are introduced to deceit, cultism, and the pursuit of power at any cost. It delves into the dark intersection of politics and the occult, where wealth is gained through sinister means, and power is maintained through betrayal and bloodshed. It examines how society enables impunity, how silence makes us complicit, and how, in the end, history is rewritten to turn villains into heroes.

But at what cost? When the sins of one generation become the curse of the next, who truly pays the price?

This fictional story does not offer answers nor provide solutions. It is a mirror held up to a nation fighting with its own demons. It is a warning, a revelation, and, perhaps, a call to those who still believe that change is possible.

— *Faith Ose Ebhodaghe*

CONTENTS

1

The signpost on the door read "Hostel One." It was slightly bent to the side. Aza Kio Briggs, a fourteen-year-old boy, stood at the entrance with his luggage. He glanced at the paper in his hand, realising he was at the right place. He nodded.

Just as he was about to step inside, a smaller boy, about his age, walked out of the room, drying his tears with his sleeve. His shirt was drenched with sweat as he passed by. Aza, surprised, watched as the boy strolled down the passage, struggling to hold back more tears. Peering into the room, he caught a glimpse of one side of it: a row of beds stretched to the far end. The windows, thick with dust from countless school terms, were partially shut.

From where he stood, he could hear students laughing. Periodically, the sound of a whip descending on a body cut through the noise. Aza shivered. He tightened his grip on his luggage handle and stepped inside.

The door creaked open. Instantly, the once noisy room fell into dead silence, as though everyone had seen a ghost. All heads turned towards the entrance. Shocked by the attention, Aza glanced behind him, hoping they were fixated on something else—anything but him.

"Ah! Another new boy", a student almost twice Aza's size, said, accompanying it with a laugh.

"Goo… Good… afternoon," Aza stammered.

"It's evening, olodo," another boy, the same height as Aza but well built, sneered. All the boys in the room laughed.

Aza noticed a fair-skinned boy carrying a desk while on his knees. Around him were a few students who definitely looked older and taller than the rest. He tried to keep his gaze away from the circle but couldn't help but notice the bruise on the boy's temple and the way his hands trembled, as though they were about to give up and let the desk fall on his head.

Terrified as he locked eyes with a muscular boy in the circle holding a whip, Aza threw his gaze to the floor. He quickly scanned the paper in his hand for his bed number, 'Bed 8.' Immediately, his eyes met bed 8. It had a new mattress. Unlike the other beds, it had its own little cupboard. He smiled as he rolled his luggage to the bed, but stopped abruptly when someone stood in his way.

"No! No! New boy, that's not your bed."

"That's the number given to me by the principal," Aza protested.

"Then go and get another number from him." The room erupted in laughter.

Aza stood there, confused. He looked around and noticed that the boy with the whip was now watching him keenly. He turned back to the boy blocking his way.

"But that means we'll be disobeying the principal if I don't get my bed."

The whole room burst into laughter again, except for one boy in the corner, his head buried in a sheet all this while.

"Who cares? Boy, don't be stubborn. You surely don't want us to teach you how to be obedient," the student threatened.

Aza scanned the room again, hoping to find an empty bed. His eyes landed on one in the corner. It was far from any windows, leaving the area almost dark. He sighed and weaved his way through the littered room.

"Is this taken?" Aza pointed to the upper bunk. He waited for a response from the fat boy lying on the lower bunk, his face still buried in the sheet.

"No, it's free," the boy replied, his voice muffled.

Aza took off his school bag and threw it onto the bed. He began unpacking his luggage, carefully taking out each item. There was an old, damaged shelf near the bed, and he noticed its lock was broken. He pulled a spare lock from his bag and tested it on the shelf. It worked. Satisfied, he continued unpacking—placing his beverages and biscuits neatly inside. He took some money from the side pocket of his school bag and squeezed it into his pocket. From the corner of his eye, he noticed that the boys were watching him. He froze.

"You've made a whole lot of scenes on your first day," the fat boy said from the bunk below. His bunkmate, Clement, was now up and was seated on his bed.

"What do you mean?" Aza asked.

"You could have walked into the room silently."

Slowly, the noise that Aza's presence had once stolen began to creep back in. He turned to look at the boys, all of whom had returned to whatever they were doing. His eyes landed on the boy holding the whip.

"That's Jude, the hostel prefect," Clement said, noticing Aza's confusion. "He sleeps on the bed you were claiming." He paused. "He's someone you don't want to cross paths with."

Both boys continued watching as Jude and his clique assigned a new punishment to the boy on the floor.

"Next time, when a senior calls, you answer," they heard Jude say as he whipped the boy.

Jude suddenly looked up, and Aza and Clement quickly turned their gazes to the wall.

"That's it, I'm off," Clement said, picking up his little bag and hurrying out.

Aza followed, feeling Jude's gaze upon him.

"Wait, where are you off to?" Aza asked once they were outside.

"To get a drink from the kitchen."

Realizing he hadn't introduced himself, Aza stretched out his hand with an awkward smile. "I'm Aza. Nice to meet you. What's your name?"

Clement paused, looking like he didn't know what to do with the outstretched hand.

"I'm Clement," he said, finally grabbing Aza's hand. He hesitated. "I'm also new here. I resumed two days ago."

"Well, it seems like you've learned a lot about this school already," Aza joked as he walked away with Clement.

The next morning, still dark, the room was already busy with boys coming and going, towels tied loosely around their waists. The screeching of pale iron buckets scraping the floor and the sharp smell of antiseptic filled the air. Two boys walked in, completely naked, engaged in a heated argument about a football match scheduled for that afternoon.

Jude comes in. Another boy follows with his bucket. He points to where he wants it placed, and the boy hurries to put it down. Jude scans the room. Everyone is busy arranging their uniforms, everyone except one person. Aza.

Aza jolts from his sleep, breathing heavily. Jude has just emptied a bucket of water for him. He wipes his face and the frown that would have put him in more trouble.

"Do you think you are in your house where you get to sleep as you like?" Jude shouts, threatening to pour more water.

Aza jumps off his bed, still surprised. He looked at everyone in the room. They all paused to watch him. It's another day, and his presence seems to exude a lot of drama since he arrived.

Clement entered the room, holding his sponge and toothbrush. Shocked at what was happening, he stopped, upset that the water had also reached his bed. He murmured something inaudible.

Jude turned to see the dazzled boys staring at him and Aza.

"What? Don't just stand there and look," he shouted to the boys. Immediately, they shuffled back to what they were doing. He looks back at Aza. "What's your name, New Boy?"

"A...A...Aza"

Jude laughed.

"Listen Aza, here, there is time for everything, time to sleep like a fool and time to wake up. Understood?"

Aza mumbled.

"Understood?" Jude barked again.

"Understood!" Aza replied.

"Now get out of here."

Aza picked up his bucket and reached for his toothbrush. He hurried to the bathroom, freezing when the water touched his body. It was ice-cold. He knew asking the kitchen staff for hot water wouldn't just be difficult. It would take a lot of time and almost certainly incur Jude's wrath again.

He had barely washed himself when he heard someone banging on the bathroom doors. He went dead silent, refusing to pour water now so he wouldn't attract whoever it was.

The banging moved from door to door, growing louder as it neared his stall, then it stopped.

Aza exhaled in relief. Whoever it was must have turned back.

Feeling alone, he scooped water and poured it over his body. Immediately, a loud bang rattled his door. His heart skipped a beat. The banging resumed. This time, harder, angrier.

"Who's there?" It was Jude's voice. "Get out before I come in there and pull you out."

Aza poured the last of his water, hurriedly grabbed his things and walked out of the bathroom, avoiding eye contact, knowing the hostel prefect's gaze was still on him. From afar, he heard Jude burst out laughing. Unknown to Aza, he still had soap on his head as he walked away, struggling with his bucket.

When it was 7 AM, the sound of the bell came again. Then students began to leave their rooms and walk towards the kitchen. Clement signalled to Aza as soon as he stood to leave.

"Are you not coming?" He asked.

"Hold on," Aza quickly threw the bottle of moisturiser he held into his bag. He removed his wet sheet and picked up a cloth peg to dry it once he got out.

"Where is everyone going?" Once outside, he asks Clement.

"We have our breakfast by 7:15 AM," Clement said, pausing to check his watch. "The cafeteria is where everyone is headed now."

The cafeteria was a large hall, three times the size of their room, with tables and benches as long as minivans, arranged in rows and columns. Each boy had to sit facing another while turning his back to the next.

A kitchen master stood at the entrance of a door leading to an inner room, where the food came from. Jude and some other seniors had entered this room, their laughter echoing across the hall.

The kitchen master barked orders to the staff, who moved swiftly, some carrying trays filled with loaves of bread, others holding large jugs, pouring them into each boy's cup. He pointed to different sections of tables, directing staff to serve hungry children waiting on the benches.

"Why does it taste like this?" Aza asked Clement. He had yet to recover from the porridge he had last night before bedtime.

"Like what?" Clement said, almost halfway into his meal.

"Isn't it supposed to taste better?" He stirred the tea with a plastic spoon. He took a sip from the spoon. "No sugar."

"You better eat and don't let them know you hate food." Or else that will be your last meal in this kitchen," Clement said, pointing to the kitchen master, who was seated, listening to a commentary on the upcoming electoral campaign on the radio.

"You seem to know a lot already."

"I had a rough start too," Clement shrugged, narrating his ordeal to Aza.

Just like Aza, Clement had had a rough start on his first day. The fat kid had refused to do the laundry of a senior student and was told to run around the school field with a gallon of water.

He finished his meal and got up from the table. Aza signalled to him to wait on while he finished up his. Hesitantly, Clement sat back down, waiting till his friend finished swallowing his meal. Then the boys walked to the assembly ground to join the other students.

It was just past 4 AM on Sunday, and Aza lay wide awake, waiting for the morning bell. He had always been fascinated by the precision of whoever was responsible for ringing it. Staring at the ceiling, he whispered his morning prayers when a cool breeze slipped through his blanket, sending an unexpected sensation through his body. His arousal grew, intensified by the crisp morning air. The feeling was almost electric, unfamiliar yet impossible to ignore. Instinctively, he reached down, finding a strange sense of pleasure in the motion.

Just as he became lost in the moment, the bell rang: 4:30 AM. Without hesitation, Aza sat up, the lingering temptation still pulling at him. But he remembered the other day—Jude's cold-water wake-up call had taught him a valuable lesson—the risk wasn't worth it. He jumped and ran to the bathroom to wash himself. He came back and dressed for church. Unlike his regular uniform, Sundays had a different outfit, which most students preferred to the housewear that made them look like jailbirds.

Aza's first Sunday at Montgomery Boys College was nothing like he had imagined. The service was at a catholic church, and he was thrilled by the change of scenery—especially the presence of girls.

He had never considered that being surrounded solely by boys could become so tiresome. When he transferred from a day school to a boarding school, he had envisioned days filled with endless football matches. But reality had been far different, and he was already growing weary of it. Seeing the girls at church brought a sense of excitement. Though it also stirred something more unsettling within him. The tension from that morning returned with unexpected intensity, pressing uncomfortably against his trousers. He tried to hold it down discreetly, but the pain was unbearable.

Just then, a firm tap on his shoulder snapped him out of his trance. Turning around, he found himself face-to-face with Jude, the hostel captain.

"Where do you think you're going?" Jude asked sharply. "Can't you follow the line?"

Aza hadn't even realised there was a line. He had been so lost in his thoughts that he hadn't noticed anything around him. But just as quickly as it had come, the tension faded. After all, hearing Jude's voice could make anyone go cold. Scanning the line, he spotted Clement, who had saved him a space. Together, the students walked into the parish, with Jude already reserving some pews for them to sit.

The mass was progressing beautifully, and Aza found himself drawn to the choir. Their voices were so melodious that, for the first time, he considered joining. Just then, a girl stepped forward to grab the microphone. She wore a soft pink gown, her hair elegantly pinned back beneath a small cap, reminiscent of those worn by British monarchs.

She was stunning.

As he continued to watch, something else returned—the same unbearable tension from before. This time, it surged through him with such force that he had no choice but to leave the mass, rushing to the restroom.

Inside the restroom, he battled with his conscience. You're in church, for God's sake. But the urge was overwhelming. Despite the guilt gnawing at him, he gave in. When the release finally came, so did a wave of shame.

As Aza stepped back into the church, he felt a pair of eyes on him. Glancing across the hall, he spotted Jude watching him from a distance—his expression unreadable, but his side-eye unmistakable.

As they filed through the school gates on their way back from church, gunshots suddenly rendered the air.

Aza's first instinct was relief—they were back on school grounds. Had the attack happened while they were outside, the chaos would have been unimaginable. But his relief was short-lived. Panic erupted as students scattered, racing towards their hostels for safety.

Amid the frenzy, a piercing cry cut through the commotion. Aza turned just in time to see Clement collapse to the ground, his white shirt rapidly staining with blood.

For a moment, Aza froze. While everyone else was running for their lives, he stood rooted to the spot, torn between dashing to safety and going back for Clement. His mind raced, but his feet wouldn't move.

Then, without warning, a strong hand yanked him backwards.

"Run, you fool!"

Snapped out of his daze, Aza bolted, sprinting as fast as his legs could carry him. He was the last to reach the hostel. As soon as he stumbled through the gates, Jude slammed them shut and locked them behind him.

Spinning around, Jude glared at Aza, his face contorted with anger.

"You want to die, abi? I should have left you there to die with your friend!"

Aza's face held no expression. His mind still raced back to Clement, who must have bled to death. He raised his head to look at Jude, who was now standing before him, probably waiting for his appreciation. Not only had he not realised earlier that it was Jude who dragged him during the chaos, but he also did not realise that he had bruised himself when he stumbled through the hostel gates. He felt the need to go back and check on Clement, hoping he was only hallucinating when he saw him bleed. He made for the door but Jude shot him a stern look, stopping him immediately.

He looked around. Everyone was quietly sitting on their beds, waiting for the chaos outside to end. Some very dramatic juniors lay flat on the ground with their hands on their heads. One of them had already peed on his uniform. He just lay there covered in shame other than urine.

After a while, they couldn't hear any sounds. The gunshots from the police had stopped, and the entire place was silent except for the sound of footfalls cutting through their window from the bush path nearby, which a short fence separated them from. Jude instructed all the boys to stay indoors while he went out to check what happened.

That evening, Aza hoped Clement would return, maybe with a bandage, but undoubtedly alive. Things felt slower when the hostel prefect returned before dinner. He had gathered his clique around him, and they were playing cards.

"Do you guys know that fat boy is dead?" he said without a tiny bit of empathy.

Aza, taken aback but still in disbelief, walked up to the group. He had abandoned his clothes, which he was folding.

"What did you say?" he asked. Realising he sounded authoritative, he took a step back in preparation for an unexpected attack from one of the boys. "I am sorry. Please tell me what you said." He asked again.

Jude barely looked up at him, ignoring the new boy. He kept on throwing cards on the bed while his friends hailed him.

"Your fat friend didn't make it. He is dead," he said. He had played his last card and now turned to look at Aza, who was now staring into everything but nothing, completely lost.

Jude snapped his finger in Aza's face, jolting the boy back to consciousness.

Aza turned to leave. He felt a tightness over his chest. His first Sunday at his new school ended in tragedy—the death of his only friend. That evening, at dinner, while the boys were feasting on yam with egg sauce, the Principal announced the passing away of a new student. The room went silent, but not long before everyone returned to their plates. Aza, concerned, stared at his meal, finding it very hard to swallow.

Rumours spread quickly. Word had it that the police had fired shots into the air to disperse a crowd while escorting a government minister. But none of the students could make sense of it. Everyone knew politicians moved with heavy security, but why was shooting into the air the only way to control a crowd? Aza couldn't wrap his head around it.

Back at the hostel, the boys whispered among themselves when Jude walked in on them.

"What are you guys talking about?" he asked.

Christian, a senior student, responded. "We heard the stray bullet that killed Clement came from the police officers escorting a minister, but we don't know if it's true."

Jude scoffed. "Where did you hear that nonsense? It wasn't the police. It was rival cultists."

Aza's frustration boiled over. "Really? Then where were the police when this was happening in broad daylight?!" His voice was sharp, laced with anger he could no longer suppress.

Jude stepped closer, sneering. "And who exactly are you mad at? If you have a problem, why don't you go and report it to the police? Or maybe... you'd rather join your friend. When you see him, tell him to run faster next time."

Aza's breath caught in his throat. He couldn't believe what he had just heard.

"You act like you're happy he's dead," Aza snapped.

Jude stopped in his tracks and turned back. "Are you talking to me?"

"Yes."

Jude narrowed his eyes. "Repeat what you just said."

Aza didn't hesitate. He repeated himself, steady and unwavering.

In an instant, Jude shoved him to the ground. "Are you mad?"

Laughter erupted from the boys. Ebi, a student one class ahead of Aza, smirked. "Honestly, Jude should have left him to die with his friend."

Jude shot Aza a cold glance as he walked away. "I'll deal with you soon."

It's been weeks since Clement's death. Aza still found it difficult to make new friends. He was just getting to know Clement before his demise.

A day after his death, his parents visited the school with an ambulance. It was an emotional scene. Clement's sister, also as fat as he was, cried her eyes out as they carried her little brother into the white and red Mitsubishi van.

The Principal had a lot on his hands. His ironed t-shirt looked like something they had dragged out of a bottle by the time Clement's mother was done pulling at him. The fat woman had wailed in the Principal's office. She was very loud and everyone at school heard her.

Her husband, a smaller-looking man, had tried comforting her, but to no avail. Instead, she shoved the helpless school Principal, demanding why they were so careless.

It was at this moment Aza felt more connected to the family, even though he was just seeing them for the first time. He really felt pity for them while he wiped his teary eyes.

A few days before their exams began, Aza was reading on his bed when he fell asleep with his notebook. He woke up to a sharp, stinging pain across his cheek. His eyes fluttered open to find Jude standing over him.

Still dazed, he pushed himself up. "Why did you slap me?"

Jude's expression grew grim. "Are you deaf? Didn't you hear me call your name?" He approached Aza and sized him up. "And who do you think you're raising your voice at?"

Before Aza could respond, another slap landed across his face.

Fury surged through him. Much had changed since Clement's death. He had rarely spoken to Jude or anyone in the room. He no longer saw Jude the way he had when he first joined the school, nor did he see him the way Jude wanted to be seen. Now, he felt an urge to challenge him whenever he was bullied.

Without thinking, he shoved Jude back.

For a brief moment, Jude looked stunned as he staggered. The entire room froze. Boys turned to watch, whispers spreading from different corners.

Aza could see Jude's clique rising in defence. He stepped back, putting a reasonable distance between himself and Jude. One of Jude's friends made a move to attack Aza, but Jude swiftly stopped him, signalling them to stand down.

Then, the entire room erupted in an uproar as Jude began rolling up his sleeves.

Aza knew then—it was going to be a long day.

Fortunately for Aza, he was quick to avoid the first blow thrown at him, but the second came unnoticed, smacking him right on the chin. He staggered to a bunk, but his ego picked him up faster than he did to himself.

Swiftly, he launched at Jude, his shoulder colliding with Jude's stomach, pushing him till a bunk stopped their path.

Jude let out a *Yelp!* He bent low and tried to shove Aza off his belly, but the shorter boy was adamant.

After a few attempts and a yell from the spectators, Jude let his elbow thud into the middle of Aza's back thrice. This broke Aza's spirit and shook him out of his grasp as he bent so low to avoid the fourth collision. Jude hissed, yanking him off. He picked a bucket from under one of the bunks and threw it towards Aza, catching him by the chest.

Aza screamed in pain. He tried looking for an object big enough to hurt someone like Jude. But before he could completely scan his environment, Jude had gripped his neck. He pushed him to the wall, banging the short boy so hard that Aza thought the back of his skull must have split open. Then it happened so quickly, the last blow that brought him to his knees. Jude pulled him out, grabbed him by the waist and, in milliseconds, threw him to the floor. He fell so hard that he almost couldn't hear the cheers in the background except for the sound of his body hitting the hard floor.

With this defeat, seeing that his opponent could barely get up, Jude quickly yanked off his belt and lashed Aza with it. Aza didn't flinch. He was managing to get to his feet while staring at Jude with cold defiance. That only enraged Jude further.

His gang closed in, two of them shoving Aza to the ground. He tried to resist, but they were much stronger. The next moment, belts rained down on him from all sides. The sharp, biting pain blurred into one long, relentless assault. He covered his face, making sure the lashes didn't meet his face.

The other students stood there in awe. One made an attempt to run out of the room, not in a haste to report, but out of fear of witnessing the brutal scene.

At some point, Aza lost track of time. His body felt numb. By the time the first round of whipping was over, he had grown accustomed to the sting, his skin raw but his spirit unbroken.

Ebi, one of Jude's loyal followers, leaned in and whispered something. Moments later, they dragged Aza outside the hostel, dumping him onto a heap of gravel near the washing area, just by the clotheslines.

Dazed, Aza opened his eyes to find Jude towering over him once more.

"Crawl!" Jude ordered. "Up and down! Fifty times!"

Aza stood motionless, his mind reeling at the sheer cruelty of it. Before he could process the command, Ebi shoved him forward. He fell face-first onto the jagged stones, his skin scraping against the rough surface.

"If you don't start crawling," Jude's voice rang out, "I'll drag your face all over that gravel myself."

Gritting his teeth, Aza dropped to his knees. He wanted to pick up the gravel and hurl them at the faces of the seniors. He wanted to do it so badly and watch each of them bleed from their eyes and nose, but he was outnumbered, and his strength couldn't defeat all of them, so he gave in to their command. He crawled up the heap, then back down, using his palms for support. Each movement sent fresh waves of pain through his battered body.

The scene had started to gather onlookers, and they watched in silence. Aza saw a teacher watching discreetly from afar. Immediately, he turned to make eye contact. The teacher vanished as fast as he could.

By the tenth round, blood stains streaked the gravel—from his body.

At the thirtieth, another senior muttered something to Jude. Moments later, Jude finally relented. "Stop!" he ordered.

Aza tried to stand, but his legs buckled beneath him— every attempt to rise ended with him collapsing back onto the ground.

Two of his classmates, Jerad and Emoike, advanced. Without a word, they hoisted him up, supporting him as he hobbled back to his bed.

His knees bled for a long time before the wounds finally clotted. But the pain—that would linger.

Sitting in the exam hall, Aza felt so much pain. His mind was blurred; the words ripped themselves out of the paper, floating before his eyes. He had called his mother multiple times, trying to explain the torment he was enduring at school, but she never fully grasped the depth of his suffering. She would always joke about how new he was to the boarding system, telling him that the longer he stayed, the better he would adapt.

Reporting to the hostel masters had been useless. Their response was always the same, "Next time, respect your seniors."

Aza had seen some seniors punished for bullying juniors, but when it came to Jude and his minions, the rules didn't apply. Teachers, hostel prefects—no one wanted to be involved. It was as if Jude had an invisible shield protecting him from consequences.

Worse still, anyone who dared to report him suffered even more.

He had heard from some students that Jude was the son of the Inspector-General of police. On a few occasions, he had seen Jude's father visit the school with uniformed men and gave out wads of naira notes to the principal and some of the teachers he was familiar with. The first day he saw Jude's father go inside the principal's office together with his escort and Jude, he thought the hostel prefect had committed a serious crime which warranted a man to come into the school with the police. He had assumed the bully would be arrested and the entire school freed from his torment.

His class three session ended on August 13, 1993, and students vacated the school for the holidays. Aza sat by the school gate, clutching his suitcase, waiting for his mother. For the first time in four months, he felt a flicker of joy, but it was mixed with anxiety—he dreaded showing her his report card or his body that had marks as though it was some sort of map.

Later that evening, the sound of his mother's Peugeot approaching filled his ears. Tears stung his eyes, but he blinked them away. He didn't want her to think he was unhappy or broken. But as she stepped out of the car, he saw the excitement on her face melt into anger.

"What's all this on your body?" Her eyes roamed over his visible bruises. She was shocked, touching the scars. "Kio, who did this to you?" She placed the back of her hand on his neck, turned his head sideways and stepped back to take a better look at her son. "You have grown very lean," her voice was shaky. She pulled him by the hand and started marching towards the principal's office. "We're going to see your principal right now."

Aza hesitated. Quickly, he said, "Mum, the school is closed. The principal's office is locked. Let's just go home." He lied.

She looked at him again, her expression softening. "What happened?"

Only when he promised to tell her everything on the way home did she agree to leave. As he narrated his ordeal, his mother sat in silence, filled with self-guilt and regret. She insisted on confronting the school authorities when the new term started, but Aza begged her not to. She suggested she change his school, but Aza didn't like the idea of a new school. He was already getting to his senior year and knew Jude and his clique would be out of the school soon, which meant less worry for him in the school. He promised to stay out of trouble, even though he knew the trouble came to you. He just couldn't bear to see his mother embarrassed in front of people who feared a teenage boy simply because of his father's status.

Resuming his first senior year was a relief. Jude had finally graduated, which meant Aza could breathe.

On a Tuesday morning, he was studying in an empty classroom when whispers outside the window caught his attention. Peeking out, he saw a small group of seniors huddled together. Among them were Festus, Cleron, Joe, and a familiar face, Vincent, who sold cold drinks in the school compound. On some occasions, he saw Jude and his friends skip class to spend time in Vincent's mother's store, either playing cards or gambling.

Aza leaned back to avoid being seen but stayed close enough to eavesdrop.

He heard them mention Jude's name multiple times. This poked his interest.

He moved closer, making sure they had no idea someone was by the window. He heard Vincent instructing them. He strained his ears harder to listen to what he said, but he still couldn't pick up everything.

He peeped through the window and saw Vincent pointing at some of the students while Cleron wrote down something on paper, which he handed to Vincent. He saw Vincent turn sharply to leave. Immediately, he ducked, hoping Vincent didn't notice any movement at the window. After a minute, he poked his head back to see the group still discussing. This time, they sounded more audible than before, and he could hear Cleron tell them that Jude just sent a message through Vincent.

From the chatter, Aza detected their plan to help carry out electoral malpractice.

He shrugged, wondering why students had so much interest in the election. Just then, he heard something that surprised him—the amount each of them would get paid. He slid down, realising that was three times his pocket money for a term. So, he decided to join in.

Later that day, Aza approached Cleron, the only senior student ever kind to him. "Cleron, can I talk to you?"

"What's it?" Cleron said.

"I need some extra cash," he said without hesitation.

Confused, Cleron asked, "I don't have anything to give you."

"Then let me work for it," Aza was persistent. He saw confusion on Cleron's face. "Look, Cleron, I know you guys have some jobs to do this election. Let me join you in running errands during the elections. You can count on me."

Cleron was shocked. He hesitated. "What are you talking about?"

Aza chuckled, a smirk appearing on his face, "C'mon, Cleron, you don't have to deny this. Don't worry. Your secret's safe with me. All I need is a quick way to make extra cash, that's all." He stared at Cleron, who could no longer feign his denial.

"You can't do a job like this, trust me."

"Why?"

"You're a good boy. This… isn't your kind of thing."

"Come on, I can handle it," Aza insisted.

After some back and forth, Cleron agreed but promised to keep Aza's involvement a secret from Jude—for obvious reasons.

That night, Aza lay in bed, torn between excitement and fear. He had never been involved in anything like this before. He had no idea what to expect.

Aza was asleep when a Cleron tapped him. He turned in his bed, hoping the person would leave. Cleron tapped him again, harder.

Annoyed, he jumped down from his bed, only to have the frown on his face vanish as soon as he realised it was Cleron.

"Meet me at Eagle Square by 8 PM. Don't be late."

Aza simply replied, "Okay." He didn't ask questions—he already knew this had to do with the elections.

He laid back on the bed but couldn't get any sleep again. He was nervous. *Would Jude be there?* That would be a disaster. His last encounter with Jude left him with a scar. A part of him wanted revenge so badly; another part was still scared of the thought of Jude.

He checked his time to see how long he had left to wait before scaling the fence at the back of the hostel, which led to the location where he would meet Cleron and the rest of the boys.

He arrived at Eagle Square early enough, and minutes later, Cleron arrived with a group of older students. Then, out of nowhere, Jude showed up.

Aza, tensed, still tried to put up a little bit of boldness but was careful enough not to hurt Jude's ego. He noticed Jude was surprised to see him amongst the group, readjusting himself as Jude walked to him.

Jude came up to him. Without saying a word to him, he turned to Cleron. "What is this fool doing here?"

Aza felt struck. He would have liked to retaliate, but that would have been costly. Right now, his relationship with Jude will determine whether he will be chosen for the job. If he got off on the wrong foot, Jude wouldn't just deny him access to the money, he might even beat him up without anything to stop him.

Cleron defended him, "We needed more hands for the thumbprinting, and he asked to join."

"You didn't think to tell me first?" Jude sounded livid.

Before Cleron could respond, a fat man whom everyone called Bishop walked in. Oblivious to the ruckus already building up, he began explaining the task. We would be taken to a location, given ballot papers, and instructed to thumbprint them. Payments would be handled by Jude.

Aza wasn't comfortable with the arrangement, but he had no choice. He needed the money.

The night before the job, Jude received a message from Bishop. There's been a change of plan. The job was now on Friday at 4 AM. He decided to inform Ebi but intentionally left Cleron and Aza out. He sent a message through the drink vendor,

Vincent, since he and Jude were fond of meeting in town, telling him to inform Ebi and lie to Cleron.

Jude already knew Vincent would ask questions, so he told him that he suspected there was a mole and that Cleron had no idea that Aza was there to help the opposition party. So, he instructed Vincent to tell Aza to wait at the school farm for the driver, who was to hand him some ballot papers.

On Friday morning, Aza skipped class and went to the school farm to find the driver already waiting. He handed a bag and a folded piece of paper to Aza, who discreetly took it back to his hostel, hiding it from the eyes of other students.

He opened the folded paper, and it was the location where he was to drop off the bag. He squeezed it into his pocket and sneaked out of the school with the bag through the back of the hostel.

Once the school walls were out of his sight, he picked to his heels, panicking. He was almost behind time and was scared that someone would want to stop him on the road.

He reached the supposed drop-off point, realising there were no students there, not even Jude. He turned to see if anyone had followed him. At that moment, two police officers came from a bend around the path he had used, and Aza froze with the bag. They walked towards their parked van, talking about the election. Aza walked back, realising he hadn't caught their attention. Immediately he thought he had paced a good distance from the duo, he turned to run.

"Hey! You! What are you doing over there?" One of the officers called out. Aza thought his heart fell to his stomach. He walked slowly, attempting to leave the bag behind.

The second officer called out. "What's in the bag?"

Aza hesitated. He thought about running but knew it was pointless. He turned back. His face showed disappointment.

His mind raced to a million things he could have been doing rather than attempting electoral malpractice.

He thought of his mother. He had hidden enough from her, all the bad habits he had picked up in school. This will be the straw that broke the camel's back. If he is sent to jail, she would definitely know, and this would change how she perceived him—her innocent son.

He thought of the other boys who were supposed to be here. Have they been caught also? Why didn't any of them show up?

"Open it!" One of the officers instructed, interrupting Aza's thoughts.

Slowly, he unzipped the bag with trembling hands. The officers watched him closely, immediately grabbing him by the waist after realising what it was. One of the officers walked close to him and stared keenly. He had a moustache and a peculiar smell that made Aza's nose cringe.

"And na small pikin oo," the officer said.

"Na dem dey do bad, bad things pass," the second officer said. He was ransacking the bag they had collected from Aza. "See wetin dem dey use dis pikin do."

"Where you come from?" the moustachioed officer asked.

"Mo... Mon... Montgomery Boys College." Aza answered.

"So you be student wey suppose dey school now?"

"Yes sir."

The officers stopped to look at themselves. They shifted to discuss something. The moustachioed officer spoke while the other nodded. Once done, they returned to Aza, who was almost in tears.

"Oya enter car make we dey go your school. Today nah your lucky day. Nah say you still small or else you for don sleep for cell today."

Aza joined them in the truck, dead silent as they drove to the school.

Meanwhile, Jude and his group were busy thumbprinting ballots at the abandoned town hall.

Cleron, sensing something was wrong, turned to Jude. "Are you sure Aza is coming?"

Jude smirked. "If he hasn't changed his mind." He walked around, supervising the other students who were buried in the task.

IMPUNITY

2

The Principal's office door creaked open, snapping him out of his thoughts. The secretary, a lady whom the students always called Corper, stood in the doorway, her expression unreadable.

"The Principal will see you now," she said.

Aza stepped inside, his pulse racing. The Principal, who had just escorted the policemen to their car, regarded him sternly before delivering the verdict.

"You are to leave the school premises immediately. Your mother will be contacted once a decision has been made regarding your future in this school."

Aza went down on his knees, tears welling in his eyes.

The Principal, seething with fury, pulled out a whip from behind his chair, making Aza's heart pound. In a flash, he bolted out of the office, startling the secretary, who was scribbling something into one of the large books that filled the administrative office.

He hurried to the hostel and stuffed some clothes into his backpack.

It was afternoon, and the students were busy having lunch, giving him the perfect chance to slip away unnoticed. He left in haste, abandoning some of his belongings.

Now, he had to find a solution before news of his suspension reached his mother.

On his way home, Aza thought about Jude and how the Principal had treated him with such care, as if he were fragile. If he could convince Jude to sway the Principal's decision, maybe he had a chance.

He stopped in his tracks, turned down a side road, and headed back to school. If he had to reach Jude, there was only one person who could help him—Cleron.

To avoid being caught by the Principal, he took the back route, where a short wall separated the hostel building from the town. With practised skill, he climbed over and landed back on school grounds.

By now, the students had returned from lunch. He set off to find Cleron, who was surprised to see him.

"Aza! What happened?" Cleron asked.

"I need your help. I was caught with the ballot papers and have been suspended. I need to contact Jude to help me out," Aza said hurriedly, glancing over his shoulder to avoid the hostel masters.

Cleron looked confused. "How am I supposed to help you with this?" he asked.

"Where does he live?" Aza asked, quickly squatting at the sight of his hostel master.

Cleron hesitated, but guilt gnawed at him. A part of him felt responsible for letting Aza in. With a sigh, he pulled out a piece of paper, scribbled something on it, and pressed it into Aza's palm.

"Don't mention that I gave this to you," he warned.

"I won't," Aza promised before scurrying to the back of the hostel building, the same way he had come.

Now, he was headed to the address Cleron had given him.

Knock, knock.

He knocked again, but there was no answer.

Growing impatient, he tiptoed to the side of the house, peering through the window. The room was empty. *Where could he be at this hour? It was nearly dark.*

Deciding to wait, Aza paced around the house. As he reached the back, his breath caught at something deeply unsettling.

Behind the toilet area lay a sack—bulging, ominous. Nearby, a machete, a hoe, and other digging tools were haphazardly strewn about, their blades stained with what looked like blood.

His stomach twisted. "Is that… blood?" he muttered.

Before he could process the thought, a shadow loomed over him.

"Jude?"

Faster than Aza could react, Jude seized him by the throat, his grip tight, his voice a furious growl.

"What the hell are you doing in my house, sneaking around?" he snarled. "Are you stupid? What do you want?"

"Jude, please, listen to me," Aza pleaded. "I'm not here to cause trouble—I just need you to hear me out. I swear, I don't know what happened. I followed your directions exactly. I don't understand how I ended up with the police."

"You almost ruined our plan, you idiot."

"How was I supposed to know that the police were there? I was arrested and returned to school. The Principal suspended me."

"Did you mention any other person's name?"

"No, I was asked, but I told them I was alone."

Jude was impressed but didn't show it. "Well, that's your problem. Now, get out." He shoved Aza towards the gate

Aza followed but stopped. He turned back to Jude and gave it one more shot.

"Please, Jude," Aza begged. It was his last choice. "I am in serious trouble right now. Only you can help me out."

Jude's eyes narrowed. "By the way, what the hell were you doing at the back of my house?" His voice dropped to a menacing growl. "Get. Out. Now."

"I'll do anything you ask," Aza said desperately. "I was caught with the ballot paper and given an indefinite suspension. I know you have the influence to keep me in this school. I… I… I don't want to go home, Jude. I beg you—whatever you want, I'll do it."

Jude studied him for a moment, then smirked. "So, will you do anything?"

"I'll do anything," Aza repeated, his voice trembling. "I can't afford to be expelled."

"I can help you, but not until I get the permission to do so." Jude waited, staring at Aza, who was curious to understand what he meant.

"From who? Why do you need to ask anyone?" Aza questioned.

"Because there are certain privileges reserved for those who belong to the group of friends," Jude responded.

"Does it cost much to belong to this group of friends?"

"Not really. You just have to meet with them, and you become one of us," Jude said. He waited anxiously.

Aza glanced at his watch—it was already late. He looked at Jude, who gave him a nod, expecting a reply.

"If you have nothing else, then you can start going," Jude said, pointing towards the gate.

Aza hesitated. "Okay, I am willing to join the group if that's all it requires."

Jude glanced around to ensure no one was watching before nodding toward the door. "Come inside."

Aza wasted no time stepping in. Jude walked over to his bar, pulled out a bottle of gin, and poured himself a drink. Then, turning to Aza, he asked, "Do you drink?"

"No."

Jude smirked. "How do you plan to belong to a group that drinks if you don't drink?"

"I do... just not often," Aza replied hesitantly, then almost immediately added, "I'll have a glass."

Jude poured another drink and handed it to him. "Now, tell me—what do you really want?"

"I need you to talk to the school authorities. I just want to stay, that's all I ask."

Jude leaned back against the counter, swirling his drink. "And you said you're willing to do anything in return?"

"Yes. Anything."

Jude chuckled. "All right then. Tonight, there's a gathering at Nile Centre where you will get to meet my friends—those who will always help you once you get into trouble." He paused to gulp down a mouthful of his drink. "You will have to go over there and meet with Cleron."

"Meet with Cleron? That's it?" Aza asked, surprised.

"Just do what I said. No questions," Jude smiled mischievously. "Yeah! That's all."

"Fine. And after that?"

Jude took a long sip from his glass. "Depends on how far you're willing to go."

Aza didn't hesitate. He stood up, his nerves on edge. *Was this really all Jude wanted, or was there more to it?* He didn't know. All he knew was that he had to stay in school, no matter what.

"What are you waiting for? Go," Jude commanded. He gulped down the last swallow and went into his room, while Aza walked out, dashing to the Nile Centre.

The path to the Nile Center was a long one. Aza, nervous, had his head filled with so many questions that he could have asked, but he didn't want to upset Jude. He checked his watch—it was already very late. Fear crept in as he thought about going back home, and he prayed that the Principal hadn't reached out to his mother yet.

Soon, he reached the path he dreaded most—a narrow bush path flanked by almond trees on both sides. The last time he had taken this path was during the daytime, and then, he had no reason to be afraid. This time, it was different. From afar he could hear a cacophony of whistling pine trees and the hooting of owls. He shivered, sticking to the middle of the path to avoid the trees.

He had heard stories about snakes using the trees as their bedroom at night. Now, he was almost walking on his toes, making sure to move as quietly as possible so as not to attract the so-called snakes. Carefully, he crossed over a fallen tree log along the path. Once he was out of the narrow passage, he hastened his steps, noticing the fading sound of vehicles from the road he had just left behind.

He turned back, realising that, at this point, he had already walked far from civilisation. He hissed, muttering a curse as he moved on.

Everything was beginning to look strange. The last time he came here, the path had seemed much shorter and far less intimidating. But tonight, it felt like he was a character in some horror movie.

As Aza made his way deeper, the faint sounds of passing cars had completely faded. Now, only the chirping of crickets and the hooting of owls filled the night. He noticed flames flickering in the distance.

Rounding a bend, he came upon a road with a wire mesh gate. Although it was locked, he could get through by slipping into the shallow ditch beside the gate pillars. He jumped in and emerged on the other side.

After walking only a short distance from the gate, he heard the crackling sound of dry twigs burning. Relief washed over him—Cleron must have arrived before him. He quickened his pace, almost running, until he reached a clearing.

There, near the fire, was a group of boys.

A second glance at the fire sent a shiver down his spine. The boys lay beside it, their movements slow and deliberate. Something about it felt very off.

Maybe he was overthinking.

Shaking off the unease, Aza tried to spot Cleron. He scanned the faces from afar.

Just then, Jude appeared from behind, startling him. He was with Cleron, who seemed just as surprised to see Aza.

"Wh…what are you doing here?" Aza asked. His eyes darted to Cleron and then back to Jude. "I thought I was supposed to meet him," he said, pointing at Cleron.

They both walked past him without a word, heading towards the rest of the boys by the fire.

"Why are you still standing there?" Jude called out.

Aza ran to catch up, wondering if he had made the right decision by coming here. He knew for sure that it was already too late to walk back the way he had come—going alone down that path in the dark wasn't an option. And if he backed out now, he wouldn't get any help from Jude. He had no choice but to do what he was told.

"Hey, just be nice. We'll be out of here soon," Jude said.

Moments later, a deep, resonant clang echoed through the air.

The group was unusual. Aza had expected friends who would be chatty, drinking, gambling, and probably even have girls around. But here he was, trying to blend in with guys who just silently stared at a fire while a gong kept sounding.

It felt like an initiation.

"Step forward," a voice commanded.

Jude nudged Aza, urging him to move. Hesitantly, he took a few strides forward—only then did he realise he had stepped into the centre of the gathering.

A tall, imposing man eyed him critically.

"Do you know where you're standing?" the man asked.

Aza shook his head. "No."

A cold wave of fear swept through him. A part of him wanted to turn and run, to leave everything behind. But where would he go? He couldn't navigate that eerie path alone, and backing out now would mean losing Jude's help for good.

He had seen movies where certain groups of friends took their bonds seriously—so seriously that they swore oaths to be true to each other. This must be one of those groups.

He lifted his gaze, searching for Cleron, hoping for reassurance. But Cleron kept his head down, deliberately avoiding eye contact.

Before Aza could react, someone shoved him to his knees. His heart pounded as Jude called out to a man they referred to as Bishop—a high-ranking member of the group.

Without hesitation, Bishop marked Aza's face, chanting and dancing around him. Aza was still trying to grasp what was happening when a sudden blow landed at the back of his head, nearly knocking him out. Before he could react, fists and feet rained down on him with relentless force.

He was more confused than in pain.

Fifteen minutes later, he lay on the ground, barely conscious. His entire body throbbed, his vision blurred. Blood pooled in his mouth, thick and metallic. He coughed and spat, the taste bitter on his tongue.

"What... what did I do?" he croaked. "Why are you doing this to me?"

A tall, masked man loomed over him.

"You are now Yhesus," the man declared. "Your life belongs to us. You must abide by the laws of the group. Any violation... will have consequences."

Aza's stomach churned as the realisation hit him—he had just been initiated into a cult.

He lay still, his breath ragged. *How did I get here? Why did I come?*

Then, through the haze of pain, a familiar voice broke through.

"Aza, get up! We need to leave, now!"

Jude's urgent tone barely registered in his pounding head.

Cleron rushed to his side, grabbing his arm and trying to lift him. Aza hesitated. A part of him wished they had just finished him off. But his survival instinct won. Weakly, he let Cleron support him as they staggered away from the clearing.

When they arrived at Jude's apartment, Cleron hurried back to school, bidding the duo goodbye. He slipped into the hostel unnoticed, while Aza remained in Jude's, trapped in his thoughts.

Standing under the shower, Aza let the water run over him, groaning in pain. He shivered as the warm stream washed away the blood, his skin stinging with every drop. He bit down hard, trying to suppress the agony.

He wished—desperately—that he could wake up and find this night had been nothing but a nightmare. But reality clung to him like a shadow.

How did this happen? Am I really a cult member now? All because I needed a favour? Was this worth the two years I have left in this school?

His fists clenched, anger and regret twisting inside him.

Why would Jude do this to me? How do I get out of this?

He knew the Yhesus group could be tied to something far more sinister. But maybe—just maybe—he could use it to his advantage.

He stepped out of the bathroom, still nursing the pain that clung to every inch of his body. His head throbbed violently, his limbs felt like dead weight. Too weak to stand, he sought a chair, but the pain was unbearable. His legs gave out, and he dropped to his knees.

Crawling forward like a wounded animal, he inched toward the sitting room, hoping to reach the sofa. Each movement sent fresh waves of agony through his body. His vision blurred, the world around him tilting. Then, his legs refused to move. The pounding in his skull grew unbearable, swelling like a drumbeat inside his head. He shut his eyes, hoping to regain his strength.

When he opened them again—nothing. Just a flood of blackness.

His breath came in slow, ragged gasps. His chest tightened, the air thinning as if the room itself were closing in. A chilling realisation gripped him—he was losing consciousness. And then, everything went dark.

By the afternoon of the next day, Jude instructed Aza to return to school, assuring him that everything had been taken care of. Sceptical but with no other choice, Aza made his way back.

As he entered the school grounds, he unexpectedly ran into the Principal, who stood outside, inspecting a section of the roof that had been damaged since last term. The older man let out a frustrated hiss.

"Aza, how are you?" he asked, his tone surprisingly warm.

"I'm fine. Good morning, sir," Aza replied, keeping his voice neutral.

He trailed behind the Principal, his thoughts elsewhere. Inside the office, the Principal set his bag down, shuffled through some papers, and settled into his chair. Aza barely paid attention. He wasn't nervous—he already knew why he was there. The real question was what Jude had done to make this possible and what price he would have to pay next.

The Principal cleared his throat. "Aza, I'm sure you're aware that your suspension has been reversed."

Aza nodded silently.

"Someone pleaded on your behalf," the Principal continued. "Your name has been erased from the blackbook— you have no more issues. But let this be the last time you get involved in anything questionable. If you're caught in any illegal activity again, you'll be expelled permanently. No second chances."

Aza simply nodded. "Thank you, sir. I'm really grateful."

Rising to his feet, he bowed slightly to show respect and left the office.

As soon as he entered the hostel, all eyes turned to him. Students stared, their expressions filled with curiosity and speculation. It was obvious—the news of his suspension and the scandal had spread like wildfire.

Ignoring their gazes, he walked straight to his bunk and began unpacking his bag.

The morning was cold after the night's heavy downpour. The entire hostel buzzed with activity—except for Aza, who remained in bed. Now, in Class Five, skipping classes had become routine for him. If he wasn't lying back in the hostel, he was sneaking over the fence to run errands for Jude.

Today was the weekend, and the room was filled with boys doing their laundry. Aza turned on his bed, too lazy to get up.

Just then, Vincent walked in. Without hesitation, he headed straight for Aza and leaned in.

"Jude wants you at his house after lunch," he whispered.

He didn't linger. The moment the message was delivered, he left.

Aza didn't respond. He lay there, unmoving, frustration bubbling inside him. Then, with an angry hiss, he threw off his blanket and jumped down from the bed, muttering curses under his breath.

After lunch, he left for Jude's place. There was no time to process the urgency in Vincent's words. He threw on some clothes, sneaked out of the hostel, boarded a taxi, and within minutes, he was at Jude's doorstep.

Inside, the atmosphere was tense. Jude, Cleron, and two other guys sat in silence. Aza recognised them from the Nile Center.

"What's going on?" Aza asked, his gaze landing on a set of masks resting on the sofa—the same type used in robberies.

Jude barely looked at him. "Get that. We need to leave now," he said, pointing to a bag sitting on the chair.

"I don't understand."

"You don't need to understand," Jude snapped. He walked up to Aza, so close that they could feel each other's breath. Poking Aza's chest, he hissed, "Your job is not to understand. Your job is to do what you're told."

Aza hesitated but eventually picked up the bag without further questions. As he lifted it, he frowned—it was heavier than expected. What's in here? he wondered. Watching the boys out of the corner of his eye, he unzipped the bag just enough to peek inside. His stomach twisted. Money. Lots of it.

Before he could react, Jude dragged another bag into the room—the same one Aza had seen at the back of his house. One of the guys immediately stepped forward to take it.

"I think that's all," Jude muttered.

One of the guys sprang to his feet. "Guys, we need to move."

Aza glanced at Cleron, who gave him a quick nod. Something about this felt off. But before he could ask, Jude's sharp voice cut through the air.

"Let's go!"

As they rushed toward the front door, gunfire erupted. Bullets ripped through the air, forcing them to dive for cover.

Aza's pulse pounded. "What is happening? Who are those people? Why are they shooting at us?"

"Shut up!" one of the boys growled.

Another reached into a bag, pulling out guns and distributing them. Jude thrust a pistol toward Aza.

Aza recoiled. "I—I don't know how to use a gun."

Jude's glare was ice-cold. "Then go and hide. Or you die."

Aza's eyes darted around, searching for a hiding spot, but there was nowhere safe. The gunfire outside grew louder.

Then, Cleron crept up beside him, nudged him toward a door, and whispered, "Get in."

Aza didn't think twice. He slipped inside and crouched in the darkness, his breath shallow.

For five agonising minutes, the gunfire raged on. Then—silence.

Only when he heard the shooters drive off did he finally step out, his heart pounding against his rib cage. He swallowed hard at the sight before him—bodies sprawled across the floor, each lying in a pool of blood.

Aza's hands trembled as he inched forward, his eyes flickering between the lifeless forms and the black sack beside one of them. His mind screamed at him to leave, but his body felt frozen in place.

Then, a phone rang.

The shrill sound cut through the eerie silence, making him flinch. His gaze darted around, startled to see a landline telephone sitting in Jude's apartment.

Aza stood paralysed, horrified. His instincts screamed at him to run, but something held him back. *Should I pick it up? Should I call the police?*

His eyes flickered to the bag Jude had dragged in from behind his house. Curiosity gnawed at him. He took a hesitant step forward, reaching for it—.

Ring!

The phone blared again, jarring him. He hesitated, letting it ring out, hoping the caller would stop. But they didn't. The ringing persisted, relentless.

Aza clenched his fists, steeling himself. He had to decide.

Taking a deep breath, he picked it up.

"Hello," a deep voice said. "Are you with the body?"

Aza froze. His throat tightened. "What body?" he managed to ask.

The voice sharpened. "Who am I speaking to?" A pause. Then, more forcefully, "I said, who am I speaking to?"

Aza's gaze darted to the black sack. His palms grew clammy. *Say something—anything.* But before he could think, the words slipped out.

"A…A…this is Aza."

The moment he said it, regret crashed over him. He had just given away his name—his identity.

Silence. Aza's pulse pounded. *Had the caller hung up?* He held his breath.

Then, the voice returned.

"You are the new boy," the man stated. "Where is Jude?"

Aza swallowed hard. His voice barely came out. "Th…th…there w…was a shootout. He didn't make it."

Another pause.

"What about Cleron and the others?"

"They're d…dead too," Aza stammered. "It's just me."

More silence. Then, the voice hardened.

"Listen. This is Yhesus3. I am sure you've heard of me."

Aza stiffened. *Yhesus3?* He had heard the name whispered before—always in hushed, fearful tones.

"Yes, sir."

"Good. I'm going to tell you what to do, and you will do it. No questions. No mistakes. No one else must find out. Is that clear?"

"Yes, sir."

"Now, grab the bag of money and hide it in the toilet. Nothing must go missing, or I will make you regret it."

Aza's hands shook. "Okay, sir."

"Get a piece of paper. Write this address down. You will bring the black sack there by nightfall. Do not open it. Do you understand?"

The voice was sharp, final.

"Yes," Aza whispered.

The call ended.

Aza stood frozen, the phone still pressed to his ear. His heart hammered in his chest. He turned to the black sack, dread pooling in his stomach.

What had he just gotten himself into?

Aza heaved, struggling to catch his breath. His hands trembled as he wiped the sweat from his forehead. He felt foolish—reckless even—for revealing his name. Now, Yhesus3 would have him marked. Running wasn't an option anymore. Not when even Jude had been terrified of the man.

"I've messed up," he muttered under his breath.

Determined not to make another mistake, he grabbed the bag of money and hurried into the toilet, shoving it behind the door. His fingers clenched around the black sack. It felt heavier now, like the weight of his choices was pressing down on him.

Without wasting another second, Aza slipped out through the backdoor, sticking to the shadows. His heart pounded as he moved swiftly, distancing himself from Jude's apartment. He needed to make sure no one saw him.

Crossing the road, he hailed a taxi. Sliding into the back seat, he placed the sack firmly between his legs, gripping it tightly.

As the taxi pulled away, they cruised past Jude's apartment. A small crowd had gathered. Police sirens wailed in the distance, growing louder. Aza's pulse spiked, but he kept his face blank, his gaze locked forward.

A few kilometres away, he asked the driver to stop. As he stepped out, his stomach twisted—there was blood on his shirt. His breath hitched. He swore under his breath and quickly ducked into an unfinished two-storey building by the roadside.

Climbing to the top floor, he crouched near the ledge, watching from a distance. His heart sank as he saw bodies being wheeled out of Jude's apartment.

He exhaled sharply, wiping his face with his palm. It's over for them.

Exhausted, he let his body sag against the cold concrete and shut his eyes.

Sleep came fast—too fast. And with it, a nightmare.

In the dream, someone found him. They pointed at him, their voice sharp with accusation. "You're carrying human body parts."

Aza jolted awake, his body drenched in sweat. His chest heaved. The nightmare clung to him like a second skin.

His hands fumbled for the sack. It was still there. He exhaled.

Checking the time, he realised it was almost 9 PM. Without wasting another second, he dusted himself off and slipped into the night. He needed a taxi. He had a destination to reach—and no idea what awaited him there.

The building was nondescript, hidden in the shadows of an abandoned church. The street felt emptier than a ghost town, the kind of place where even whispers got swallowed by the silence.

Aza stood before a tall blue gate, gripping the bag like it was the only thing anchoring him to reality.

"Follow me."

The voice came from behind. Familiar. The same one from the phone call.

Aza turned. A man stepped out of the shadows, his presence as unsettling as the silence around them. Without another word, he led Aza down a narrow path, the bushes on either side swaying ominously in the night breeze.

"Who are you?"

Aza hesitated. "I... I am Aza."

The man's expression remained unreadable. "Who is Aza?"

Something in his tone made Aza's stomach twist. This wasn't a question about his name.

Swallowing hard, he answered, "Yhesus."

The man nodded approvingly. "Good." His eyes dropped to the bag. "Is that the body?"

"Yes."

"What really happened to Jude and the others?"

"They're dead. We were attacked."

The man didn't flinch. "And you survived." He studied Aza for a long moment, then said, "Very well, then. You will take over from where Jude left off."

Aza blinked. His throat went dry. *Take over?* "Umm… yes, sir."

"Good. From now on, you're in charge of Jude's group. You'll meet the members soon enough. Be at Ogoni Village by 8 AM tomorrow. We have work to do."

He paused. "You can call me Yhesus3."

Aza exhaled shakily. "Okay."

"Okay, what?"

"Okay, Yhesus3."

The man smirked. "Good."

Then, without another word, he stepped back into the shadows and vanished.

Aza didn't wait. He turned and bolted, his heart hammering against his ribs.

This was it. The beginning of the end of his secondary

school education. One decision, one night, and his life had spiralled into something he had no control over.

The next few years blurred into a cycle of running errands, taking orders, and sinking deeper into the world he once feared. By the time he graduated from university in 2001, he was no longer the boy who had hesitated to pick up a gun.

Small jobs turned into bigger ones. And before he knew it, he was no longer just surviving in the shadows—he was controlling them.

By then, he wasn't just in the game. He was the game.

IMPUNITY

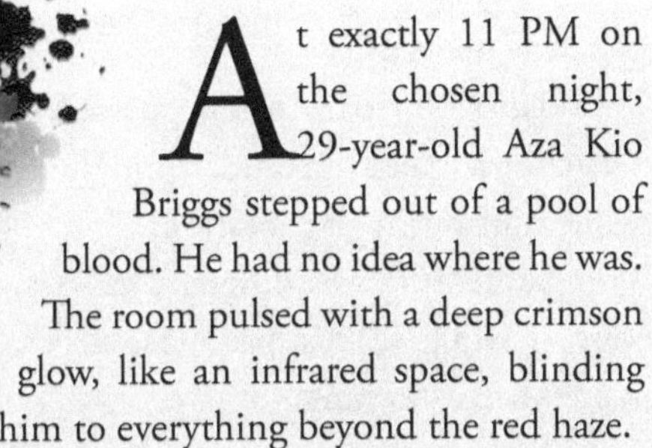

3

At exactly 11 PM on the chosen night, 29-year-old Aza Kio Briggs stepped out of a pool of blood. He had no idea where he was. The room pulsed with a deep crimson glow, like an infrared space, blinding him to everything beyond the red haze.

Then he felt it—his own skin, slick and warm. He was naked, blood trickling down his body. Standing beside the pool, he closed his eyes and exhaled.

Back then, he had told himself he just didn't want to be expelled. But the truth had always been there, buried beneath denial. He wanted power—Jude's power.

He could have asked anyone for help, but he had chosen Jude. Why? Because deep down, he had been desperate. Desperate to claw his way out of bullying. Desperate to own the system, to control people.

Now, he had it—power and wealth.

As Aza took a step away from the blood, an aged man emerged from the dark. His eyes were unreadable, his presence eerily calm.

Without a word, he raised a mirror and held it in front of Aza. He saw his own reflection—saw the man he had become.

He didn't flinch. He didn't hesitate. He took the mirror and hurled it against the wall, watching it shatter into a thousand shards.

"My name is Aza Kio Briggs!" he declared, his voice cutting through the silence.

The old man studied him for a moment before bending down and measuring a fine white substance from his bag. He sprinkled it around Aza's feet, then spoke in a foreign tongue.

"Stay there."

He obeyed.

Time blurred. An hour passed, maybe more. Then, the old man stepped forward, sprinkling water over Aza's body while murmuring incantations.

Something was different for Aza, he felt like an empty slate, having all his past erased. He knew nothing, and remembered nothing.

"Who are you?" The old man's voice broke the silence.

Aza dropped to his knees, bowing without thought. He wasn't in control anymore. Something else had taken hold of him.

The old man repeated, "Who are you?"

Silence. Then, on the third command, Aza spoke, as though he was under a spell.

"I am Yhesus10."

The old man murmured an incantation—a final seal of approval. Then, without another word, he pointed to the door, signalling him to leave.

Outside, the night breeze was cold, striking his bare skin without mercy. A few steps away from the building, still clinging to his body in a bid to shield himself from the cold, he turned around, confused, until he caught sight of his car.

He couldn't remember how he had got there or how he had arrived in this place, hidden deep within a forest. He instinctively reached for his car key, forgetting he was naked. Disappointed, he walked to the car to find his key stuck to the front wipers. He picked it up and looked around, wondering if anyone was watching. Taking a spare set of clothes from the car, he dressed quickly and sped off.

Aza got home in a hurry and jumped into the bathroom, almost slipping in his haste.

Tonight was important—very important. A high-profile party, filled with politicians and dignitaries. The kind of place where real power shifted hands. That was where he was headed.

At the venue, he walked straight to Mr Jonathan Idu, a governorship candidate.

"I have all the necessary information for you," Aza said smoothly. "I've gone through the bank's security files, and I know exactly how many people have paid."

Mr Jonathan's face remained unreadable, but Aza could see the flicker of interest in his eyes.

"Good," he finally said. "Send me the details." He gave Aza a pat on the shoulder as he passed.

"I will."

Aza spotted his boys—Barikor, Justice, and Gregory—at the bar, laughing over drinks. He smiled.

He clears his throat. "What's up, guys?" Aza greeted them.

Barikor raised his glass. "oga, greetings to you. You missed a lot—this place is crawling with pretty girls."

Justice smirked. "One sweet babe will be here soon. You'll like her. I reserved her for you."

"Good." Aza grinned, settling onto a stool by the bar. He scrolled through his phone as he ordered a drink.

Across the bar, a woman sat alone—light-skinned, with full breasts and striking curves. She had an aura of innocence, something different from the usual crowd.

Aza tilted his head, intrigued by the way she sat there alone without company. He breathed into his palm, adjusted his tuxedo, and walked up to her.

"Hey, pretty girl with the banging body, how are you doing?" he said.

The woman turned to him with a sharp, almost disgusted look—like he had something foul on his face.

Aza frowned. He was going to try again. "Why would someone with a body and looks like yours be alone at a party?"

Seconds passed before she finally muttered, "Hey."

"What's your name?" he asked.

She narrowed her eyes. "Why do you want to know?"

Aza's irritation flared. He hated being questioned, especially by a woman.

"I said, what's your name?" His voice edged with frustration.

She held his gaze, unflinching. "Why are you asking?"

Aza chuckled, now amused. This one had guts, he thought to himself.

She swallowed the last of her drink and stood to leave, fed up with the conversation she had endured with Aza.

Aza blinked. Then he burst into laughter. "Hey! Whore, are you walking away from me?"

She ignored him.

Barikor, watching from afar, walked up. "Omo, did that girl just walk away from you? She doesn't know that nobody walks away from Yhesus10."

Aza smirked, still staring after her. "Maybe she thinks that big ass of hers gives her an edge."

"So what?" Barikor scoffed. "That's disrespectful. Who the hell is she?"

He turned to the bartender. "That girl—the one who just walked out. Who is she?"

The bartender glanced over his shoulder. "She's a regular. Always here."

Aza leaned back, swirling his drink. "Just a regular."

He stood up. "A regular, giving that kind of attitude? Excuse me for a second."

He was already a bit tipsy and tried to steady himself. Agitated, his hands trembled—she had just trampled on his ego, and he couldn't sit this one out.

Outside, she turned back when she sensed someone behind her, then hastened her steps.

"Hey, regular," Aza shouted from behind.

She turned back, her brows knitting together. "Excuse me?"

"You refused to give me a name, so I can address you as I please." He had finally caught up with her. "How can a prostitute have such an attitude?"

"Excuse me? Do you know me?" she snapped.

"I don't need to know you. What else would someone who isn't a prostitute be doing in a bar at night?"

"You are a stupid man. If I'm a prostitute, then so are you."

Aza laughed. "I don't even know why I'm speaking to a whore like you."

"What did you just call me?" she demanded, her eyes blazing. Without thinking, she punched him in the face.

Aza, livid, shoved her against the wall. She stumbled, but before she could regain her balance, he pushed her down again.

He wanted to step back, but he couldn't. She tried to stand up, but Aza pushed her to the ground again. Pressing her head against the floor. She tried to scream, but he punched her hard, leaving her half-conscious.

He dragged her into a corner and stripped down her jeans. She struggled, but her strength was no match for his. He flipped her to face him. Ripping her underwear out of the way, he checked her with two fingers before thrusting into her. Her body became weaker, charged with pain, with every dry penetration. Crying, she started begging him to stop, instead he mounted more pressure on her, nearly choking her.

She wailed, but no one heard her as the club noise was too loud. Her cry for mercy didn't stop Aza either. He wanted to reach a climax. He couldn't at first, so he picked up the pace as she continued to cry.

Finally, he stood up, leaving her half-dressed on the floor. She wept, scrambling for her jeans as he adjusted his belt. He spat on the floor and walked off. He heard her curse him, but he didn't look back.

Returning to the club, Barikor met Aza.

"Boss, where have you been? Did you go after that girl?"

Aza smirked, straightening his shirt. "Yeah. Had to teach her a lesson she won't forget. Next time, she'll know how to be nice."

Before Barikor could respond, Jonathan Idu spotted Aza from across the room and strode over, his expression impatient.

"It's been half an hour. Where's the stuff?"

Aza brushed past him. "Give me a minute. I'll be back."

Jonathan's glare followed him, but Aza didn't care. Something felt off. He looked composed, but his mind was in turmoil. His hands trembled slightly. He needed air.

Minutes later, Aza returned and handed Jonathan an envelope. "Once you input the address, all the funds in the National Youth Fund Organisation account will be transferred to you."

Without another word, Aza left the club. He didn't tell his friends. He got into his car, his hands still shaking. It wasn't guilt. It wasn't regret. It was fear.

Back home, as he settled, his phone buzzed. It was Jonathan.

"Have you spoken to Yhesus3?"

"No," Aza answered.

"Call him. He has something to tell you."

"Alright."

He tossed his phone aside and sank onto the bed. Sleep felt distant. His mind refused to quiet down. Just as his eyelids grew heavy, his phone rang again. His mother.

"Hello, my son."

"Mum? Why are you still awake?"

"Why wouldn't I be? I haven't seen you in years. When are you coming home? All you do is send money."

Aza sighed. "Mum, I'll visit soon. Just relax."

"You said that last year. I need to see you, Aza. I need to know how you're really doing."

"I told you, I'm fine."

"There are things I need to tell you, but not over the phone. Come home."

Aza hesitated, then finally muttered, "Okay."

He leaned back on the couch, the dull hum of the television filling the silence. His three-bedroom bungalow was more than a house; it was his sanctuary—a temple where he could drown in his own thoughts. He rarely invited anyone over, and tonight, like many nights before, he let sleep claim him in its cold embrace.

The next morning, Aza dialled Yhesus3 to update him on the governorship campaign for Jonathan Idu.

"Did you call Sylvester Rashnok about the loan proposal?" Yhesus3 asked.

"Yeah, I did," Aza replied.

"And? What did he say?"

"He said he'd get back to me."

"Keep me posted on whatever he says. We need to move fast. I've already handed the posters contract to one of the boys."

Aza grunted in acknowledgement and ended the call.

Since joining the cult, sleep had become a distant luxury. Nightmares haunted him, making every night a battle. The bed he lay on felt like an arena where unseen forces dragged him into darkness.

Yet, he had learned to live with it.

He was hungry and couldn't wait for the meal he had ordered. He made himself a cup of tea and took some slices of bread, which he buttered.

As he ate his breakfast, his phone buzzed. Sylvester Rashnok.

"Hello," Aza answered.

"I've been calling about the loan," Rashnok's crisp British accent came through the line.

"Yeah, I know," Aza said, trying to mask his impatience. "What's the update?"

"I haven't gotten the green light yet, but as soon as I do, you'll be the first to know."

Aza clenched his jaw. The delay was beginning to piss him off. The collateral for the loan was massive—prime lands the government had agreed to transfer to the Lebanese authorities. It made no sense that the approval was taking this long.

Rashnok was a key figure in the Lebanon Congress, an entity notorious for securing lands in exchange for loans. It was an old game, a cycle that had repeated itself for years. The lands served as collateral for their business expansions.

Lebanon wasn't the first to play this hand, nor would they be the last. Initially, they had considered China for the loan, but China's demands had been too steep. Lebanon had been the easier choice.

After exchanging a few more words with Rashnok, a knock on the door pulled Aza's attention away.

His meal had arrived.

Just as Aza was about to eat, his phone rang again.

"Hello?"

"It's time for the meeting," Yhesus3 said before sending him the address.

Sighing, Aza abandoned his meal, quickly showered, dressed, and walked out. For a brief moment, he felt the urge to pray—but to whom? Yhesus or Jesus? Once, he had been a Christian, but that was a lifetime ago. Now, it didn't matter.

By 10 AM, Aza arrived at the venue. Several members of the group were already there—each known simply as Yhesus, without individual identities. In this world, they recognised one another by numbers and faces alone.

He spotted Yhesus3 and shook his hand.

"We need to kick off the campaign," Aza said.

"Yes, yes," Yhesus3 gave a nod. "We begin at midnight."

Aza raised a brow but said nothing. Instead, he found a quiet spot and sat, listening as Yhesus3 laid out the details of their plan.

The meeting dragged on until 2:30 PM. The moment it ended, Aza left.

The next day, Mr Idu called his assistant. "We need to move quickly. Did you contact the guy handling the poster distribution?"

"Yes, sir. I've spoken to him."

"Good. Now, call Aza Briggs—he's in charge of the campaign activities. I need an update on his progress."

Minutes later, the assistant returned. "I just spoke with him, sir. He said he's on his way."

"Alright. In the meantime, we need to meet with the chairmen of the various communities."

"The meeting has already been arranged, sir."

An hour later, Aza arrived at Mr Idu's office. It was chaos, his staff working round the clock in preparation for the campaign. The entire building was filled with different prints of his campaign posters. Campaign pictures showed him in different attires, designed to appeal to the three major traditions. Two of his staff struggled to arrange dozens of umbrellas to be used as souvenirs. A truck parked in the compound carried loaves of bread with Mr Jonathan's face on the packaging. A small group of workers loaded a minivan with cartons of liquid soap, each labelled with "Vote IDU for Better Leadership." At the front of the minivan was a bold picture of the aspirant.

Aza was directed to Mr Idu's office by a lady wearing a yellow vest with the aspirant's face and name on it.

After a brief discussion with Idu, they drove to the hall where the local government chairpersons were gathered.

The meeting proceeded as planned—Mr Idu delivered his speech while envelopes stuffed with cash were discreetly handed out as "souvenirs."

After the speech, Aza approached Idu with a smile. "Well-rehearsed. You delivered it perfectly."

"I just hope it was convincing," Idu chuckled.

"If not, the souvenirs definitely will be." They both laughed.

"Next, we need to meet with the traditional rulers," Aza reminded him.

"Yes, that's scheduled as the second meeting tomorrow—right after our meeting with Yhesus."

"Sounds good." He lingered for a while, enjoying a few drinks before finally leaving.

Before 8 AM the next day, a knock on the door woke Aza. Peering through the window, he saw Mr Idu standing outside. *What is he doing here this early?*

Aza opened the door, and Idu greeted him with a firm handshake. "My comrade, good morning. There's been a change of plans."

"Why?" Aza asked, rubbing his eyes.

"The Eze Apara Rebisi and his council refused to honour our invitation," Idu said, his tone laced with frustration. "They claim their loyalty lies with the other political party and won't go against them. Even after I offered them an amount higher than what the opposition is paying, they still refused."

Aza sighed, unmoved. Politics was a game, and despite the money involved, traditional rulers often remained loyal to their chosen affiliations, especially when occult influences were at play.

"So, what's our next move?" Aza asked.

"I'm looking at securing support from religious leaders."

"Religious leaders?" Aza raised a brow. "And how exactly do you plan to do that?"

"Simple," Idu smirked. "We'll start by meeting with the Bishop of the Anglican Diocese, then the Bishop of the Catholic Diocese."

Later that day, Aza and Idu arrived at the Catholic church and were seated in the Bishop's office reception, waiting. Idu leaned closer and whispered, "This is the real deal. If we can win over the priest, we'll have the congregation—at least 80%—on our side."

Aza knew he wasn't wrong. The church had long been a powerful tool for influence—often more effective than traditional rulers or community leaders. He had seen firsthand how religious institutions could be leveraged to shape public opinion.

A man in a white robe left the office. "Good day. Are you here to see the Bishop?"

"Yes," they replied in unison.

"Come with me," the seminarian said, leading them through a hallway adorned with religious artwork. Paintings of saints lined the walls, each telling a story of devotion and sacrifice. The marble steps gleamed under the glow of beaming ceiling lights. As they ascended, it felt almost symbolic—like they were moving towards something divine.

At the top, they reached a balcony where the Bishop sat in an armchair, surrounded by potted flowers and neatly arranged wooden chairs. When he rose to greet them, Aza noticed a rope hanging from his cloak, adding to the aura of biblical authority.

Idu introduced Aza and explained their purpose. The Bishop listened, smiling throughout, which left Aza wondering what was so amusing.

"So, what exactly do you want from me?" the Bishop finally asked.

"We need a few minutes to address your congregation during Sunday Mass," Idu replied. "And, of course, your support in the upcoming elections."

The Bishop nodded thoughtfully. "As long as you

can assure me that you will keep your promises, I have no objections."

Idu laughed heartily. "Of course, Bishop. You have my word."

"Thank you, Father," Aza added, placing a thick envelope on the table beside the Bishop's armchair. They exchanged handshakes and left.

On their way back, Aza's phone rang. It was Rashnok.

"The loan has been approved," Rashnok said, "but we need to inspect the land being offered as collateral."

Aza smirked and glanced at Idu. "No problem. When do you plan to check it out?"

"A week from now. We'll send a representative for the inspection, and after that, we'll process the transfer."

"Sounds good," Aza replied. "I'll make the necessary arrangements."

By the end of the month, all preparations for the election had been completed, and anticipation ran high. Victory seemed inevitable. On election day, ballot boxes were secured, and any potential controversies were discreetly handled to prevent bad press.

As the results came in, they had planted members within the electoral offices to relay updates. Aza, Idu, and other executives gathered in a conference room, waiting anxiously. However, when the official figures appeared on the screen, they were starkly different from what the electoral committee had initially indicated—and they were not in Idu's favour.

By evening, the final results were announced. Idu had lost to the opposition. Yet, he remained oddly unshaken.

Aza, bewildered, approached him. "What's happening? We were supposed to win."

Idu gestured for him to sit. "Relax."

Aza sat but pressed on. "This doesn't make sense. We had everything in place."

Idu let out a small chuckle. "I was offered fifty-two million naira to step down."

Aza's eyes widened. "What?! And you're just telling me now? What is this?"

"Calm down," Idu said, leaning back. "There will be another time."

Before Aza could protest further, Idu cut him off. "This is how the game works. The whole campaign was just to pressure the opposition. You're still new—you'll understand with time. In politics, everyone wins."

Aza scoffed. "This is the kind of politics you want to play?"

"Of course."

"You could have just told me you were in it for the money."

"I'm in it for both," Idu said with a smirk. "But in this case, I get the money without having to fulfil any promises."

Aza shook his head in disgust and stormed out of the building, leaving Idu to his inner circle.

As he walked to his car, his phone rang. It was his mother.

"Don't forget your wedding plans," she reminded him.

Aza exhaled sharply. In the chaos of the election, he had almost forgotten Ann, his fiancée, to whom he had left all their wedding preparations.

Ann kept yelling. Frustrated, she kicked her Pekingese, which wouldn't stop barking. Aza, grabbing a bunch of keys from the table, stormed out, slamming the door behind him. He fumbled with his shirt buttons as he walked down the hallway, cursing under his breath.

"Yes, walk out—that's all you ever do!" Ann shouted after him.

She sank onto the bed, exhausted. Still seething, she knocked over a framed picture from their wedding night. As the glass cracked, a folded piece of paper slipped out from behind the frame.

Curious, she picked it up and unfolded it. Her own handwriting stared back at her:

"You give me joy and happiness. With you, there is peace… On this day, 4/10/2003, I was lucky to become your wife.

Love, Ann."

She let out a sharp hiss, crumpling the paper and tossing it into the corner of the room.

There were many reasons why she had chosen to marry Aza, but love wasn't one of them. For Ann, marriage had always been a gamble. There had been plenty of red flags while they were dating—enough to make her walk away. But she had ignored them, letting her judgment be clouded by the endless stream of gifts Aza kept showering her with.

From the beginning, it was his indifference toward the relationship. Once, she had to remind him they were already dating—he had absentmindedly asked her out a second time. Then came the messages and late-night calls. She had initially suspected he was seeing another woman, but instead, she discovered he spent most of his time with a strange group of men he called his 'brothers.'

She once left the relationship after he threatened to beat her to a pulp during an argument. But he always knew how to lure her back—with gifts and vacations. She knew it was never about love. His ego simply couldn't handle being dumped.

One night, drunk after an outing with his 'brothers,' he came to her house and threatened to kill her if she ever mentioned the word 'breakup' again. She had let that slide—because, after all, she had ambitions too, and he was the key to achieving them.

Being with Aza had not only given Ann a life of luxury but had also opened doors in politics, paving the way for her rise up the ladder. Now, sixteen years into this gamble, with two daughters as the only good thing their union had produced, she had found pleasure elsewhere.

Sometimes, it was in her work. Other times, in a bottle of rum. And when neither sufficed, in the touch of younger men.

As for Aza, he had built a fortress around himself, seeking pleasure between the thighs of young girls he could control.

Aza walked to the back of his house, where he had built a smaller flat for entertaining guests. It was his refuge whenever Ann decided to shake the walls with her voice. Fumbling with the keys at the door, he muttered curses under his breath, swearing to teach her a lesson—a threat he never carried out.

Just as he entered, his phone rang. It was Yhesus3.

"You'll be meeting with the King tomorrow. I've made all the arrangements."

"Okay," Aza replied.

This was it. The meeting was his ticket to securing the position of Commissioner for Works. If the board approved, his path to becoming governor over the next eight years would be set.

Inside the flat, he switched on the light—just as a shadow flickered past.

Aza froze. "Who's there?" His gaze swept the room. He could have sworn he saw someone move. Stepping cautiously into the dim corridor, he flipped on the light.

Another shadow darted across his face.

His heart slammed against his ribs as he stumbled backwards, knocking over a flower vase. The sharp crash sent him sprawling to the floor. A wave of dizziness washed over him. His vision blurred. His body trembled, struggling against the pull of unconsciousness—but he couldn't fight it. Darkness swallowed him.

Somewhere in the void, a female face appeared. Aza trembled in his subconscious, panic gripping him while his body lay motionless on the ground. Then, faintly, his phone's ringtone echoed through the haze of his mind.

His eyes fluttered open. His mind was foggy. He tried to reach his phone, but the ringing had stopped. He groaned, lifting his head slightly to check the time—it was one in the morning.

How long have I been lying here? he thought, still trying to gather himself.

Summoning the strength to move, he pushed himself up and staggered toward his room, hunched over in pain. As he collapsed onto the bed, a sharp sting radiated from the side of his head. He reached up and felt something warm and sticky—blood.

Grimacing, he grabbed a piece of cloth, pressed it against the wound, and let exhaustion drag him into a restless sleep.

The next morning, an uneasiness settled over him. His body ached, and the wound on his head throbbed, but he was alive. Yet, the image of the female figure from his subconscious lingered in his mind.

Who was she? Could she have been one of his past victims? Impossible. Most of them were already lost souls—condemned after each ritual, their spirits powerless to return. Then who was she?

He would have to speak with the priest.

Aza reached for his phone and saw he had missed several calls. He glanced at the wall clock—it was already nine in the morning. Yhesus3 had been calling.

He dialled back.

"Why haven't you been answering your phone?"

"Something came up. I'll be ready in ten minutes." Aza hung up, pulled himself up with effort, and staggered toward the door.

As he opened it, he was met with a fleet of cars parked in his compound. On the front porch stood his wife, arms crossed, confusion and frustration written all over her face.

"You were inside all along? And you ignored my knocking?" she called out.

Aza didn't respond. He was too drained to engage in another argument—especially not in the presence of Yhesus3.

His focus shifted to the group of men waiting for him. Among them was Idris, a fellow Yhesus member he worked closely with.

"Mr Aza, are you aware of our meeting today?" Idris asked.

"Yes." Aza knew how crucial the meeting was, but his mind couldn't shake off what he had seen the night before.

One of the Yhesus members studied him closely. "Are you okay? What happened to your head?"

"I'm fine. Just give me ten minutes to get ready."

As Aza stepped back inside, his mind raced. *Why was Yhesus3 here? He never attended these meetings. And how was he supposed to explain his bruised head?*

Without another word, Aza turned and stepped back into the house. His wife followed, her gaze fixed on the wound.

"What happened?" she asked, feigning concern. She was still furious that he had ignored her in front of his guests.

Aza didn't answer. He just kept walking. She trailed behind, repeating the question, but when it became clear he wasn't going to respond, she gave up.

Forty-five minutes later, they reached the King's Palace. The meeting went smoothly—especially after they presented ten million naira in a duffle bag. The King was more than reassuring. With his backing and the cabal behind him, Aza felt invincible. Nothing could stop him now—not even the devil.

From the palace, they headed to the governor's candidate clubhouse, their usual hideout for indulgence—fornication, drugs, and sacrifices.

As Aza stepped inside, his eyes instinctively darted to his favourite spot. It was empty. The image of the woman from the night before still clung to him. *Why did she appear to me? With all the rituals I've performed, why does her spirit still linger?*

Barikor, Justice, and Gregory strolled up to him, a bottle of Moët in hand, their movements loose with intoxication.

"Commissioner!" Barikor hailed, grinning.

"Yes, my comrade," Aza responded.

Laughter erupted among them as Justice poured a generous measure into Aza's glass. Without hesitation, Aza downed it in one swig. He needed to drown out the unease clawing at his mind.

"I'm just waiting for you to take your place," Justice said, leaning in. "Once you're up there, we can finally get one of us inside. It's been too long—we need to share this money."

Aza smirked as the warmth of the liquor spread through his chest.

"We certainly do," he replied.

It was late into the night. Drunk, Aza had called his driver earlier and now waited impatiently. When the car arrived, he climbed in, mumbled a half-hearted goodbye to his comrades, and slumped into the seat, hoping for a nap.

As the vehicle pulled away, his hazy vision caught sight of Yhesus3 standing at the entrance, staring at him.

Startled, he blinked. *Why is he looking at me?*

Aza rubbed his eyes and glanced back. The man was gone. He chuckled, shaking his head. He was drunk, sure—but seeing Yhesus3 through the window of a moving car? That was something else.

Aza's thoughts drifted back to the family he had left at home. He hissed at the very thought of Ann. She was trouble—always had been. But leaving her wasn't an option. His daughters wouldn't forgive him if he did, and worse, it would jeopardise his race for the governorship.

No, he had to find another way to get rid of her. Relocation.

If he sent her to the United Kingdom, it would be the perfect cover. To make it look better, he'd send one of his daughters along, claiming Ann had moved to be her guardian.

That way, no one would suspect a thing.

A fleeting thought surfaced—the agent handling the relocation. He hadn't followed up. It was too late to call now. Tomorrow morning, he noted mentally.

His second daughter would be better off abroad. His first, however, would stay back in boarding school. She was too much like him—wild, uncontrollable. Still, she didn't like him much.

When the car stopped at the house, Aza took the keys from his driver and dismissed him. Through the window, he saw Ann watching from inside.

Why is she still awake?

A glance at his watch—past midnight.

Aza staggered into the bedroom. He gradually began removing his clothes from the living room. Ann lay on the bed, seemingly asleep.

"Ann," he called, but she didn't respond.

Irritated, he raised his voice. "Ann!"

She stirred, then snapped, "What is it?"

Aza sat on the bed, his head throbbing. "I thought I saw you at the window. Why are you acting like you don't know I'm back?" His breath reeks of alcohol.

Ann scoffed. "So? Should I roll out a carpet for you?"

Aza grabbed her arm. "You will not talk to me like that in my house."

She met his gaze and yanked her arm free. "And you will not put your hands on me like that!"

A strong scent of alcohol and perfume clung to her. Aza's eyes narrowed. "Wait, did you go out?"

"Don't ask me stupid questions."

The slap came before he even thought about it. Sharp, loud, final.

But Ann didn't cower. To his surprise, she slapped him back.

Aza froze, stunned, fury surging through him.

Then they lunged at each other. Her hands went for his neck. He clamped onto her arms. Pain shot through the side of his head where he'd been injured, but he didn't stop. He forced her backwards, regaining control, and slammed her onto the floor.

Rage took over. He beat her until she went still. Then, without hesitation, he took what he believed was his right. Stripping her naked and thrusting hard, panting amidst a throbbing headache.

"She never lets me have my way when she's conscious. At least this way, I don't have to ask, " he said to himself. And still, he felt nothing.

Aza considered going to his guesthouse, but the weight of the previous day's events still clung to him. Instead, he chose the familiarity of his private bedroom. As he stepped out, he heard soft sobbing from the floor behind him. He turned back, his expression unreadable.

"Oh, you're finally awake," he said coldly. "Now you know not to talk to me that way ever again. You don't know me, Ann, and you never will."

Without another glance, he left the room, shutting the door on her. As he walked down the hallway, a new thought took root in his mind—he needed another wife. He was done with Ann. Tired of her defiance, her resistance. What was the point of having a wife at home if he had to seek satisfaction elsewhere?

Two days before his appointment, everything was in place. Aza's wife and their twelve-year-old daughter, Nioma, had travelled abroad, while his eldest daughter remained safely tucked away in boarding school. The house was quiet—just the way he liked it. His space. His peace.

Lying beside him in the guesthouse, Becky traced lazy fingers across his chest.

"I like this place better than the main house," she murmured.

"You do?" Aza asked, smiling. "Me too."

"The red hue, the large painting on the wall… it gives a majestic feel."

"I love your description," he said, turning to face her. "Let's just hope the spirits creeping around at night don't come for us."

She chuckled. "Why are you smiling like that?"

"Just admiring your pretty face." He paused, watching her expression carefully. "Becky, can you give me a child?"

Her fingers stilled, surprised. "Are you asking me to marry you?"

"If that's how you want to put it, then yes."

She raised a brow. "What about your wife?"

"Would that be a problem?"

"No, I don't mind."

"That's what I thought."

They rolled under the sheets for the third time that night, the clock creeping past three in the morning. Aza was exhausted, but he wanted to make sure he satisfied her.

The next morning, fatigue weighed on him. Before, he could go three rounds and wake up feeling as strong as ever. But now? He felt stiff.

Maybe Ann's constant rejections affected me more than I realised. But now that she's out of the picture, that won't be an issue. Even if she returns, Becky will still be here.

Shaking off the thought, he got out of bed. Today was important—his final campaign in the city before the election. He also had a meeting with the Yhesus priest, which was odd.

The priest had never requested a private meeting. Aza had always sent his offerings, and that was enough. He was grateful he no longer had to do the dirty work himself—those days were far behind him.

Stepping into the shower, he let the warm water cascade over his body, rinsing away exhaustion.

Then he felt it.

A cold hand wrapping around his torso from behind.

Aza froze.

"Can I have a bath with you?" a voice whispered against his ear.

"Yes," he responded instinctively.

Then he felt something thick trickling down his chest.

Looking down, his breath hitched—blood.

His eyes widened. He turned sharply, expecting Becky. But the arms wrapped around him weren't hers. They were skeletal, the flesh rotting away in patches.

Aza's scream tore through the bathroom.

"Yhesus!"

The grip on his chest tightened, almost crushing his ribs. Panic surged through him, and in his desperation, he screamed a name he hadn't spoken in years.

"Jesus!"

"Aza! Aza, what is it? Are you okay?" Becky was banging on the bathroom door.

Aza gasped, blinking. The shower was still running. The blood, the hands—they were all gone. He was exhausted. He bent at the waist and took a deep breath.

He swallowed hard. "Yes," he said hoarsely. "I thought I saw a snake at the window."

"A snake?"

"Don't worry," he muttered. "It's nothing."

Becky responded hesitantly, "Okay." She still wasn't convinced that a snake could make him scream that way.

Aza was still breathing heavily, his body tense from shock. He muttered to himself, This has gone too far.

He had always dismissed strange occurrences, but this? This was something else. He now had every reason to see the priest—and not later, but before the campaign began.

Stepping out of the shower, he scanned the room. No blood. No trace of what had just happened. Taking a deep breath, he walked into his dressing room, still feeling the ghostly presence lurking in the air.

Becky sat on the bed, fully dressed.

"You're dressed already?" he asked.

"Yes," she replied. "You were there for a long time. I kept hearing the shower running each time I checked on you."

Aza glanced at the clock—past 9 AM. He hadn't realised how much time had slipped away.

He called his driver, then turned to Becky. "Change of plans. You need to go home. I have somewhere to be before the campaign."

"What? Why?" she asked, surprised.

"Just do as I say and stop asking questions," he snapped. "I'll call you when I'm ready."

At the Yhesus house, Aza arrived to find Yhesus3 deep in conversation with the priest. He frowned. There was no scheduled meeting today.

71

What's he doing here? Does he have a reason like I do? Aza wondered.

Before he could say a word, the priest called out, "We were just talking about you."

Aza stiffened. He sat at a table, uneasy under the priest's piercing gaze.

"A female spirit has been hunting you," the priest stated.

Aza's eyes widened, though he wasn't surprised the priest knew.

"Yes," he admitted.

"But we don't know why," the priest continued. "Do you?"

"No," Aza replied. "That's why I'm here."

Yhesus3 remained silent, watching him intently.

The priest's voice was calm but firm. "You will be told what to do when the time comes."

"What?" Aza's patience thinned. "I can't deal with this torment for long."

"You should have thought about that before stepping out of line," Yhesus3 finally spoke, his tone sharp.

Aza turned to the priest. "What did I do?"

The priest leaned forward. "You broke your agreement."

"How?"

"You have a child with a dead woman—one no one is aware of."

Aza's heart pounded. "What? How? The only woman I have children with is my wife."

The priest and Yhesus3 exchanged a knowing look.

"You have to find the child," the priest said. "If you don't, there will be consequences."

Aza bowed his head and left, feeling even more lost than before.

A child? A bloodline I don't know about?

As he stepped outside, his thoughts spiralled. *After this election, I have to start searching for this so-called child. And to think I almost had one with Becky, outside of this covenant...*

But that could wait. Maybe she would be the one to give him a son, no matter what they said.

He sighed, his mind clouded with uncertainty. *"I've been with so many women... Where do I even begin? The ones I seduced? The ones that seduced me?"*

A hollow feeling settled in his chest. With everything that had happened in his life, he no longer knew who he was or what he truly wanted.

Just an empty soul chasing power.

As Aza slid into his car, he picked up his phone. The screen was flooded with missed calls—unsurprisingly, Becky topped the list.

She can't possibly need my attention right now.

He had no interest in calling anyone back. He was already en route to the governorship campaign ground, but his mind was elsewhere.

Who was this woman? How was she dead yet still haunting me? And worse, how did she have my child?

None of it made sense.

His phone buzzed again. He clenched his jaw, irritated.

"Drive faster," he snapped at his driver. "Why are you moving like this is a donkey ride?"

"Oga, the road is bad," the driver muttered.

"Just shut up and drive."

His paranoia was rising, but his frustration wasn't just about the road. What's happening at the campaign ground that has everyone blowing up my phone? And why wasn't Yhesus3 coming with him? He hadn't even mentioned the campaign— that was unusual. He seemed more focused on my ordeal with the ghost. And why was he so mad, like my problem was his problem? All these thoughts occupied his head.

Aza exhaled sharply. *I can't wait for this campaign to be over.*

They had been on the road for an hour and were still 30 kilometres from the venue when they came to an unexpected stop.

A police checkpoint.

Aza clenched his jaw. *Oh, for goodness' sake. These useless policemen.*

They weren't using his siren-fitted car, which meant unnecessary delays and, most likely, extortion.

He had a rule—*if someone doesn't work for me, I owe them nothing.*

"I didn't make my money for policemen," he often said.

As they approached the barricade, one of the officers signalled them to stop.

"Why you get tinted glass? Roll down your window, Oga," the officer barked.

The driver rolled down both his window and the one on Aza's side.

"Hello, gentlemen," Aza greeted, his tone laced with forced politeness. "How work?"

"Oga, this your tinted glass, you get permit?"

"Yes."

His driver handed the document before the officer could ask again. The moment they saw the name Aza Kio-Briggs, one of them perked up.

"Ah! Oga Councillor! No be you them one appoint for Commissioner for Works?"

Another officer chimed in, grinning. "Ah, big Oga! You go bless us today!"

Their faces lit up with excitement, their voices rising in exaggerated praise.

Aza barely masked his disgust. Even a fool could see he loathed their presence. But he wasn't surprised. Their behaviour was typical.

Without a word, he reached for a bundle of money, already set aside for moments like this. He handed each officer ₦20,000.

They erupted into cheers, showering him with ridiculous praises as if he were royalty.

"Safe journey, Oga!" they called as they waved him through.

As the car pulled away, Aza checked his phone again, several missed calls. *What the hell is going on?*

He quickly typed a message to Barikor.

I'm ten minutes from the location.

Then, without hesitation, he switched off his phone. No more distractions. Not until he got there.

As Aza's car pulled up at the entrance of Gowon Stadium, a commotion erupted. Becky, Barikor, and his team banged on his window. He rolled it down, his face tense.

"I'm here now, I'm so sorry..."

Before he could finish, Barikor leaned in and whispered urgently, "Have you seen the video circulating?"

Aza's stomach tightened. "What video?"

"The one from the club. The one where you talk about sharing government funds."

Aza's heart slammed against his chest. "What are you talking about?" he barked, fumbling to switch his phone back on while reaching for the door handle.

Barikor stopped him. "No. You can't get out now."

"He has to," Justice argued. "People are already leaving. He needs to say something and get it over with."

Aza's phone vibrated again, his wife calling this time. He ignored it and turned to Barikor.

"How did this video get out? Who's doing this to me?" He questioned.

Becky stood there, motionless, watching him like a mannequin. Aza shot her a sidelong glance. *Jezebel.* The thought flickered in his mind. But she wasn't at the club that night. That left only one suspect.

Greg? No, impossible. He's on my side.

His eyes darted between Barikor and Justice. *Or is it one of them?*

Justice's voice cut through his thoughts. "Aza, you have to address the crowd."

Aza's legs felt weak beneath him. He had never been in a situation like this—public disgrace waiting to unfold. He turned to Barikor.

"Let me see the video."

Becky interjected, "I don't think you should do that."

Aza's patience snapped. "I don't think you're in any position to give opinions here."

"She's right," Barikor said. "Watching it won't change anything."

Aza wasn't convinced. "I need to see it. Maybe I can twist the words in my favor."

With a sigh, Barikor pulled out his phone. Within seconds, he found the video—as if it had been at the top of his list all along. He handed the phone to Aza.

Aza's stomach twisted as he watched. The video focused solely on his face, as if he were speaking to himself. The voices of his friends were distant, barely audible, but his own voice was crystal clear.

"We certainly do need to share this money."

Aza's mind reeled. *Did I really say that?* He had been drinking, but not enough to forget. Something about the video felt off. It was edited. He was sure of it.

His eyes flicked between Barikor and Justice. There had been three of them that night. *Why would one of them betray me?*

Justice finally spoke. "I think the video was edited."

"Obviously," Aza snapped. "Why is it only my face in the frame when all three of us were talking?"

Justice bristled. "Calm down, Aza. Don't shout at me. I'm just as surprised as you are."

Barikor cut in. "None of this matters right now. You need to address the crowd—this could affect the governorship votes. Focus on what you're going to say."

Aza's breath hitched as a memory flashed in his mind—a certain governorship aspirant who had been booed off stage for lying. A cold wave of fear crept over him, but he pushed it down.

The crowd was unusually silent during Aza's speech, their expressions unreadable. He could sense their scepticism.

From the podium, he spotted Barikor and Justice approaching. His pulse quickened. *Now I understand why it's hard to distinguish friends from enemies. We pray for God to eliminate our enemies, but it's our friends we should be worried about.*

Barikor gave a small nod. "The speech was alright. I think the crowd is buying it." He turned to Justice. "I'm guessing not everyone saw the video."

Aza said nothing. At this point, he wasn't sure whether he was standing with allies or foes.

"We need to deliver the package to the community chairman," Justice said firmly.

Aza hesitated. "I'm not sure that's a good idea."

"Why not?" Barikor asked, his tone sharp. "You know without that money, you can kiss the community votes goodbye. And after what just happened, it's even more important to do the needful. Besides, we were already told to locate your team immediately after the campaign, remember?"

Aza exhaled and pulled out his phone, dialling Ese, one of his team members.

Before he could say a word, Ese answered, "Sir, can I come for the package as promised? I'm already with the chairman."

"Okay," Aza muttered.

He got into his car, signalling his driver to start moving.

"I think you both should stay here while I handle the handover," he told Barikor and Justice.

They exchanged a look, clearly surprised. Aza knew exactly what they were thinking—they expected their cut. But he no longer trusted them enough to take them along.

"Relax," he added, smirking. "Your money is safe. No need to panic."

Barikor didn't look convinced, but Aza didn't care. He leaned back in his seat and instructed his driver, "Let's go."

Aza arrived at the agreed location, spotting Ese waiting for him. They parked in an open space. Without wasting time, Aza reached into his bag, pulling out bundles of cash while his driver and Ese counted.

Then came the sound of a car speeding toward them.

Aza froze and looked at Ese. "Did you tell anyone about this location?"

"No, Oga," Ese said, shaking his head.

"So why is a car coming straight at us?"

The driver chimed in, "Maybe there are houses around."

"Houses? What stupid houses?" Aza snapped.

Before they could decide whether to leave, three vehicles came to a screeching halt, surrounding them.

Ese, startled, tried to run when he saw the police officers jump out, but he was immediately apprehended. The third van opened, and a swarm of reporters with cameras poured out.

"Oga Councillor," one officer called out. "You are wanted at the station."

"For what?" Aza asked, instinctively trying to hide the bundles of money in his hands.

One reporter stepped forward. "Sir, is that the money you stole from the government office? Were you planning to use it for the campaign?"

"What money? What are you talking about?" Aza barked.

The officer ignored him. "Oga, you and your boys need to follow us now. Or we'll use force."

Aza's legs wobbled. His driver and Ese quickly obeyed, following the armed officers. A policeman slid into the driver's seat of Aza's car while another lifted the sack of cash from the back.

The reporters swarmed, their cameras flashing, voices firing questions from every angle.

As Aza entered the police van, a cold wave rushed through him. This wasn't his first time getting arrested, but something about this felt final—less like a van, more like a prison.

At least the vehicle was fully covered. No one outside would see his face.

But his mind wasn't on his reputation. It was on the election.

"Oga," Ese said. "Are you sure you didn't tell anyone about this location? Because I didn't."

Aza glared at him. Ese had been with him for years, through dirtier situations. He should trust him.

The driver added, "I was thinking the same thing. Whoever leaked that edited video is probably behind this."

Ese hesitated before asking, "Oga, should I call Yhesus3?"

Aza's eyes rolled. *Why hadn't Yhesus3 called?*

"He's at the campground," Ese added.

Aza's face lit up. "He was there?"

"Yes."

"Okay, call him."

Ese quickly dialled. "Oga Yhesus3, we've been arrested."

Aza watched as Ese listened, nodding.

"What did he say?"

"He said he'll get us out immediately."

Aza exhaled, but the relief was fleeting.

At that moment, he wanted to call someone—his wife, his child, even Becky. But he couldn't. Sitting in the back of that van, he realised he had let his family go. He was surrounded by people, but there was no one truly by his side.

When they arrived at the station, Aza watched as officers moved in and out, busy with their duties. Spotting a familiar face, he called out, "Ah, officer."

The policeman quickly recognised him. "Oga Councillor," he greeted with a salute.

Aza felt a brief wave of relief—the officer knew him.

But before he could respond, another policeman barked an order. "Take them inside."

Their belongings were confiscated, and they were shoved into separate cells.

Aza didn't resist. He remained still, confident that he wouldn't be in there for long.

Liverpool, England

"Yes, hello?" Ann Briggs answered the call, recognising the voice on the other end.

"Hello, Mrs Ann."

"Are you aware your husband has been arrested?"

"What? How?"

"I'm still trying to gather details, but from what I heard, he's being charged with fraud. Have you seen the video?"

"I have," Ann admitted. "But I didn't think it would lead to an arrest."

"Well, I'm sure he'll be out soon," the caller reassured her. "But listen—I have some important news. The Governor is considering you for Commissioner for Tourism."

There was a pause.

"Oh," Ann finally responded, but there was no excitement in her voice.

"You don't sound thrilled."

"Of course I am," she said flatly. "I guess I could do that from the UK?"

"Possibly. But what about your husband? He's back home."

"What husband?"

The caller hesitated. "Mr Briggs."

Ann let out a humourless laugh. "Oh, him. I'll be coming home from time to time—for my daughter."

"So, does that mean you're accepting the position?"

"Yes, I'll be in Nigeria soon."

"Good. Congratulations, Commissioner."

"Thank you," Ann said. "I appreciate everything you've done."

"You're welcome to the office, ma." The line went dead.

Ann sank into a chair, staring at nothing in particular. Commissioner for Tourism… to do what, exactly?

For a moment, she had almost forgotten about her husband's arrest. But she knew he'd be out soon. *His goons will take care of it. He doesn't need me.*

She got up and rushed to the window, shutting it. This was the fifth time it had rained today, and the downpour showed no sign of stopping. The weather in Liverpool was miserable at this time of year.

Checking the clock, she sighed. *Nioma should be home soon.*

"I hope she doesn't get stuck in this stupid rain," she muttered, rubbing her temples.

Three days in the cell had been nothing short of torture. The officers weren't harsh to him, but the mosquitoes and bugs were relentless. The filth, the stench, and the uncertainty gnawed at him. *Why am I still here?*

Election day had come and gone, and he had no idea whether his governorship candidate had won or lost. One officer casually mentioned that he had lost, but Aza dismissed it as a cruel joke—he was too sure of his victory. He had tried asking about his driver and assistant, but they ignored him.

He sat at the corner of the cell when he heard voices echo down the corridor. From what he could make of their conversation, the officers were inspecting every cell. As they approached Aza's cell, he remained still, watching.

Before he could rise, the cell door swung open. A uniformed officer stood before him, smirking.

"Ahn ahn, Oga Commissioner, what are you still doing here?"

Aza couldn't answer. He had been asking himself the same question.

"Hmm, na wa o. Your people really play you," the officer said, shaking his head.

Something about the man's face seemed familiar, but Aza couldn't place him. He was still trying to recall when more footsteps approached. A warden pulled out a set of keys, and the officer gestured toward him.

"Oga, come outside."

Aza didn't hesitate. He stepped out quickly.

"Today is your lucky day," the officer said.

As they reached the front desk, one of the policemen turned to his colleagues.

"You people no remember this man? He be the one wey give us money for road three days ago. Na him be this! Why una never release am?"

The memory hit Aza. The officer had been part of a roadblock unit that stopped him on his way to the campaign ground.

Another officer immediately responded, eyes wide. "Ah, Oga! Na you? I no know o! But why nobody come bail you?"

Aza stiffened. "What about the men arrested with me?" he finally asked.

"We don release those ones since," the counter officer replied. "Dem no even sleep here."

Aza's chest tightened. He clenched his jaw.

"Abeg, come sign, make you dey go," the officer continued.

As Aza moved to sign, another officer chuckled.

"Dem say you steal money. Na true?"

Aza didn't respond. He simply signed and walked out.

Outside, the cool air hit him like a slap. He was free, but he felt like a ghost. Thankfully, he still had some money in his wallet. He flagged down a taxi and gave the driver an address—his hidden guest house.

As he sat in the backseat, his mind raced. This has to be a joke.

His fingers trembled as he switched between apps on his phone, checking the news. The headlines confirmed his worst fear.

It wasn't a joke. It was his reality. Again, his governorship candidate had lost an election.

"This is not possible!" he shouted, his voice cracking.

A sharp twist in his stomach made him double over. He felt sick, dizzy—his gut clenched so hard he almost soiled himself.

5

The school bus wheeled to a halt, its doors hissing open. Nioma jumped down in a hurry, landing lightly on the pavement.

She stood on the sidewalk, pacing as the bus disappeared down the road. Pulling out her phone, she tapped frantically on the screen. Every few seconds, she glanced up, scanning the street while trying to avoid drawing attention.

Checking the watch on her wrist, she shook her head. Too late.

With a quiet sigh, she started walking towards the junction at Overbury Street and Smithdown Lane. Then, just as she reached the curb, she stopped in her tracks.

Quickly, she texted Nate.

Nioma: I'm at the junction.

He replies almost immediately.

Nate: Me too. Where exactly are you?

Nioma: I just entered Overbury Street.

She looked up from her screen and spotted a guy—way taller than her—standing beside a red Volvo truck near the Eighth Century Church. He wore distressed denim and a brown hoodie, his hands tucked into his pockets.

Glancing around, she made sure no one had noticed either of them. But then, her eyes landed on an old lady in dark shades, staring right at her.

Nioma's stomach tightened.

She froze, her pulse quickening, then instinctively turned to walk in the opposite direction. But just as she moved, the old lady rose with a cane, tapping the ground as she walked away.

Relief washed over her.

Without hesitating, she hurried to Nate, keeping her eyes on the ground.

When she reached him, she didn't speak. Instead, she tapped his shoulder.

Calmly, he turned, a smile playing on his lips. He reached into his hoodie pocket, pulled out a small piece of paper, and handed it to her.

In exchange, she discreetly slipped him some cash.

Neither of them lingered. Without a word, they left in opposite directions.

Nioma never looked back.

As she walked, Nioma slid the paper into her backpack, tucking it between her textbooks. If she had to do this under her mother's nose, she had to do it right. One mistake, and she'd be on the next flight back to Nigeria.

When she got home, her heart nearly stopped.

Her mother stood by the couch, staring out the window.

Nioma froze mid-step

Did she see me?

The open structure of the houses and the wide roads made it easy to observe everything—especially for someone as sharp-eyed as her mother. But she wanted to believe she was in the clear. She had approached from the usual bend, the one that kept her hidden until she stepped off the bus.

Ann turned, her gaze landing on Nioma.

"Why are you just standing there? You can't greet me?"

Relief flooded through her.

"Hey, Mum," she exhaled.

Ann's gaze sharpened. She stared at her daughter for a long moment, as if trying to see past her skin.

"What is 'Hey, Mum'?" she snapped.

Nioma swallowed. "Sorry. I mean, good afternoon, Mum."

Ann raised a brow. "You mean?" she echoed, unimpressed. "How was school?"

"Fine," Nioma mumbled, already heading toward her room.

Ann didn't stop her. "Your food is in the kitchen," she called after her, already turning back to the window.

Inside her room, Nioma closed the door and turned the key in the lock. Her mother never needed an invitation—or a knock—to enter.

She exhaled, her shoulders finally relaxing.

Without hesitation, she went straight to the bathroom, turned on the tap, and undressed. As the warm water filled the tub, she slid in, letting the heat loosen the tension in her muscles.

After a few minutes, she reached into her backpack and retrieved the folded paper Nate had given her.

Unfolding it, she plucked a pill from inside and swallowed it.

Leaning back, she draped her arms over the tub's edges, eyes fixed on the ceiling.

She began to hum softly, letting the words form as they came to her.

"Looking down at the sky, two worlds divide, then they merge...

merge...

Going to school, two worlds divide, then they merge...

When you die, two worlds divide, then they merge..."

As she sang, her mind drifted.

She saw herself slipping into another universe, where the sky was a deep navy blue, and stars burned like fire. She shut her eyes—too bright, too intense. But in the darkness of her mind, another image emerged.

A woman. Ragged clothes. Lying on the ground, wailing, pleading.

A man. On top of her, moving with force, lost in pleasure.

Two silhouettes. One panting from desire, the other from pain.

Nioma squinted, straining to see their faces, but all she found was blackness.

Then, the man stood up, spitting and cursing inaudibly.

Her throat tightened. A faint curse slipped from her lips. She let out a low chuckle, mumbling the lyrics of an old song—until a scream tore through her thoughts.

"Mum!" she cried out.

A sharp voice cut through the silence.

"What is wrong with you? Why aren't you answering? I've been calling! Open this door!"

Nioma's eyes flew open.

Her mother.

Her heart pounded. Scrambling out of the tub, she grabbed her robe, wrapping it around herself as she hurried to the door.

She unlocked it and pulled it open. "Sorry, I was in the shower. I'm sorry, Ma."

Ann's expression was anything but forgiving. Her sharp gaze pinned Nioma in place.

"For how many hours?"

Nioma blinked. *How long had I been in there?*

Her eyes darted to the wall clock, but she had no memory of what time she'd gotten home.

Ann poked her head into the room, scanning it suspiciously—as if she expected to find someone hiding.

Nioma forced herself to stay calm. "I fell asleep in the tub," she said, hoping it sounded convincing.

Ann's voice turned sharper. "I've been knocking for the past thirteen minutes! What is wrong with you?"

"I'm sorry, Mum. I didn't hear you."

Ann exhaled in frustration. "I don't know what the hell you do in this room. If you're not eating your food, put it in the fridge—but make sure you eat it. Don't let it sit there till tomorrow."

Without waiting for a response, she walked away.

"Okay, Mum," Nioma murmured, shutting the door behind her. She took a deep breath, exhaled, then quickly dressed.

Slipping the key into her pocket, she left the room.

In the kitchen, Ann was microwaving a meal.

"Your food is in that flask," she said, pointing to a white container on the counter.

Nioma opened it, and the rich aroma of chicken pepper soup filled the air. Beneath the soup compartment, neatly stacked cubes of yam sat, waiting.

Her stomach growled.

Without hesitation, she rushed to the dining table and dug into the food like a starving beast—one hand gripping a piece of chicken, the other steadying the bowl of soup.

Ann watched her from behind, her expression unreadable. Then, she pulled out a chair and sat beside her daughter.

Feeling her mother's gaze, Nioma slowed down. She set the chicken back into the bowl and picked up a piece of yam with her fork instead.

"Now you know you're hungry?" Ann remarked dryly.

Nioma smiled sheepishly and continued eating.

"I'll be traveling back to Nigeria next week."

Nioma froze. "What?!" Her voice came out louder than she intended. "Why? What about my school?"

"Don't worry. I'll leave you with Aunty Tonye. She'll take good care of you—I know you like her."

Yes, she liked Aunty Tonye, with all her childish gist, but she loved her cooking more. Aunty Tonye never failed to prepare a perfectly made Nigerian dish whenever she came over. But living in a household that reeked of violence? That was something she never wanted.

"Since I'm being offered the office of the Commissioner for Tourism, I have to show up. But I'll be back."

Nioma's stomach twisted. "When?"

Ann shrugged. "When I settle into my position, of course."

Nioma hesitated. "What about Dad?"

Her mother's face hardened. "What about him?"

Nioma lowered her gaze and focused on her food.

"Your father is busy doing what he does best—chasing power. That's all he cares about."

Nioma looked up. "Are you going to fight him?"

Ann narrowed her eyes. "Why would I do that? And why are you asking?"

"Would he be happy that you're continuing in that position?"

Her mother scoffed. "Who cares what he thinks? Please eat your food, dear. This is not something you should be worrying about."

A lump formed in Nioma's throat.

As she turned her attention back to her plate, a sudden pain shot through her stomach. Nausea gripped her. The thought of her mother returning to Nigeria—to her father—made her sick.

Her father was never kind to her mother. They all knew that.

So why would she choose to work in the same environment as him? To live in the same space?

She swallowed a piece of yam and turned to look at her mother, who was now at the sink, rinsing dishes.

Their eyes met.

Ann smiled.

Nioma forced herself to smile back.

Aza had just returned from the yearly Yhesus bath—an event he never looked forward to. Though his soul was gone, a part of him still clung to the hope of redemption. Yet, he knew no life outside of Yhesus.

He walked into his house and found Becky sitting on the couch, cradling his twin daughters—again.

He had hoped for a boy.

Although Aza still kept it a secret from the public, he had let Ann know that someone else had a child for him.

Since he lost the opportunity to be appointed as commissioner, he wouldn't mind working out a divorce plan with Ann.

She had left for England and never looked back. Even during her first tenure as commissioner, she ran most of her affairs from abroad, instructing her minions at the office on what to do.

Her contact with him had grown pale over the years, but that didn't bother him.

He only made sure to keep in touch with his daughter, Nioma.

"Becky," he called out.

She turned to him lazily. "Oh, I didn't see you come in."

Of course, she knew. She just didn't care.

"They all change," Aza murmured under his breath.

He was too drunk and dizzy to argue, so he staggered towards his room. Behind him, Becky's voice trailed off—something about money. He ignored her.

After losing his chance at a political position, his finances had taken a significant hit, forcing him back into his underground dealings. It paid well, but not well enough.

And now Becky was having an attitude.

Typical. What was I thinking, bringing a whore into my house?

He flicked on the light—

And froze.

In the mirror, a shadow loomed—a figure he had seen before.

His breath caught in his throat.

Yhesus must be after me for violating the code—for impregnating someone unknown to them.

Why don't they just tell me?

Why this ghostly torment?

Aza turned off the light switch.

Then turned it back on.

The shadow was gone.

Exhaling sharply, he turned toward the shower—

And his blood ran cold.

It was there.

Standing right in front of him.

It looked like his own shadow, but the light was in front of him—there was no way his shadow should be there.

The room was well-lit.

Yet, as he turned, the shadow didn't move.

It wasn't his.

Aza felt like he had just woken from a coma.

His head throbbed, and beside him lay a shattered flower vase.

"Again?" he whispered.

He couldn't remember what had happened or how he ended up on the floor. But judging by the time on his wristwatch, he had been unconscious for about thirty minutes.

And yet again, no one had come looking for him.

He tried to move, but his body refused. His limbs felt like dead weight. So he just lay there, staring at the ceiling until exhaustion dragged him back into sleep.

The next morning, voices rattled in his brain—the sharp tone of a woman, and the wail of a child, at the sight of blood.

Aza kept his eyes shut, paralysed by fear.

The ghost.

Was it here again?

The sounds grew louder, piercing through his haze— then, a hard tap.

Aza flinched.

Slowly, he forced his eyes open.

Becky was leaning over him, one of the babies dangling from her arm.

"What happened? Did you fall? How long have you been on the ground?" she asked frantically, trying to lift him with one hand.

Aza managed to sit up, but his left arm and leg were numb. His vision in his left eye was blurred.

Becky hooked an arm around him, struggling to support his weight while balancing the baby. He could do nothing but drag himself along like a snail.

"Why aren't you saying anything?" she pressed.

He wasn't sure why either.

"Aza, talk now. What happened? Should I take you to the hospital?"

"No," he said at last.

The words came out clear, surprising him. He had feared he had lost his voice.

"Just leave me here and call my driver."

"You are not fine. Your head is swollen."

The baby in her arms started wailing, the shrill cries slicing through Aza's pounding headache.

"Take the baby out," he muttered. "I'm fine. Just call my driver."

Becky gave him a long, suspicious look, then turned and left the room begrudgingly.

Minutes later, Becky and the driver helped Aza out of the chair. He glanced at his legs as they trembled beneath him. He barely felt them.

"So, where are you going now?" Becky asked as they eased him into the car. "You need to go to the hospital."

Aza didn't reply. He had no strength left to argue.

At around 6 PM, as night began to creep over the fading daylight, Aza's driver sped down the road, pushing the car harder than usual. He never spoke during these trips to the woods—never asked questions, never showed concern.

Unlike Aza's previous driver, this one seemed indifferent.

A part of him liked that.

The car raced forward, and though the speed was unsettling, Aza felt no urge to tell him to slow down. He was too tired to care.

As they reached the dirt road leading to the woods, the car lurched, colliding with a tree trunk. The driver tried to regain control, but everything happened too fast. He stomped on the brakes, swerving to the right, but it was too late—the right front wheel struck a rock, sending the car off the road and down a steep slope.

Aza panicked, watching the driver struggle with the steering. Then, without warning, the car flipped onto its side and rolled down the slope until a tree stopped its descent.

Aza barely reacted.

It was as though time had skipped past him too quickly.

He sat buckled in his seat, his head tilted downward. The sharp scent of fuel filled his nostrils. In his half-conscious state, he saw the driver, Adamu, struggling to get out. Blood poured from a deep cut at the back of his head.

As the car settled, Adamu reached for something on the ground. He tried to break the windscreen, but his hands were too weak. More blood gushed from his wounds. Aza's gaze sharpened, noticing that not only was his head bleeding—shards of glass were buried deep in his neck.

"Adamu..." Aza's voice was barely a whisper.

The driver banged against the window, his movements frantic. The car trembled from his efforts. Then, finally, he squeezed through the broken glass, desperately trying to stop the bleeding by pressing against his neck—completely unaware of the deep gash at the back of his head.

Seconds later, Aza heard a scream. A raw, gut-wrenching cry.

It was Adamu.

Aza tried to move, to lift himself from the awkward position he was in. But before he could react, the car shifted again—this time, slamming flat against the ground.

"No, no, no!" Aza screamed. "No!"

Heart pounding, he tried to bend forward, desperate to see if Adamu was trapped beneath the wreck, but his body refused to cooperate.

He crawled towards the shattered window, dragging himself out with what little strength he had left. The cold night air hit his face as he gasped, struggling to go around the car. But no matter how much he tried, he couldn't find him.

Silence.

No cries. No movement.

Aza knew what that meant.

Adamu was dead.

A rush of helplessness crashed over him. His thoughts swirled in chaos. He could barely stand—his legs refused to hold his weight. So, he did the only thing he could.

He crawled.

Through the wet grass, through the muddy water, through the pain gnawing at every inch of his body. His wounds stung, but he didn't stop.

As he crawled up the steps of the tent, the pungent scent of burning incense filled his nostrils. From inside, voices chanted, "Yhesus." The priest and the president led the incantation with such intensity that the other voices were nearly drowned out. The sound grew louder as Aza drew closer.

They knew he was coming.

Softly, under his breath, he whispered, "Jesus."

A prayer? A plea? He wasn't sure.

With the last burst of adrenaline left in him, Aza shoved the shrine door open. To his surprise, only two men stood inside. But the voices he had heard outside—there had been more than two.

Beside the priest, a drum sat on the floor, two sticks resting on top of it. The chanting never stopped. They acted as if Aza's entrance was inconsequential.

Slowly, he crawled towards the priest, struggling to prop himself up beside the drum.

The door creaked behind him. A small boy stepped in, closing it gently before walking towards Aza. Without a word, he bent down and handed him the drumsticks.

Then, he walked to Yhesus3's side, picked up a gong, and started playing. As he struck the metal, he swayed rhythmically, his body moving in slow, deliberate motions.

The priest and Yhesus3 kept chanting.

Aza lifted the sticks and struck the drum. At first, slowly—the sticks falling on the drum one at a time—then, he picked up speed, his hands swaying up and down, lashing the drum as though it were the cause of all his torment.

The sounds clashed in chaotic dissonance—the gong in one rhythm, the drum in another, the chanting spiralling in its own erratic flow.

There was no harmony, yet none of them stopped.

Then Aza felt it.

A presence.

His pulse quickened. He turned towards the priest, searching for confirmation, but the man's eyes remained shut, his body swaying in fervent devotion. The boy's eyes were closed too. Even Yhesus3 was lost in the trance. Their movements, wild and unhinged, made them look mad.

Yet, they were in tune with the spirits.

Aza exhaled sharply and closed his eyes.

Darkness. Then heat.

Something moved around them—shadows in the form of flames.

The chanting echoed, reverberating in his skull, and then—

"Aza Kio Briggs."

His full name.

His breath caught in his throat. He tried to move, to speak, but he was paralysed.

The spirits had pulled him in.

His hands, no longer his own, struck the drum with relentless speed. The closer the spirits came, the faster he played. His shoulders ached, his wrists burned, but the rhythm possessed him. He couldn't stop.

Aza felt himself slipping away. His soul detached from his body, hovering above, watching as his flesh suffered below.

He no longer recognised the man beating the drum with inhuman speed. Not even a madman could move like that. Yet, he was powerless in this transient state, trapped in the eerie stillness of his spirit while his body was consumed by the ritual.

Around him, familiar spirits drifted, their presence heavy, their forms shifting in the dim glow.

Amidst them, he saw her.

A painfully thin woman.

Yes… it's her.

He reached out, but the closer he tried to get, the farther she seemed. Slowly, she faded into the shadows, slipping away.

Aza's focus was locked on her, his entire being drawn towards the spirit, oblivious to everything else.

Then—

"Cecilia Briggs."

A name rang out behind him, clear and resounding.

He froze.

"Mum?"

Aza tried to turn, but he couldn't. He felt himself being pulled downwards with the spirit, as though he were getting sucked into the ground—yet his feet never left the floor.

The name echoed again, growing louder.

"Cecilia Briggs."

His mother's name.

Terror shot through him.

A name was only spoken in a Yhesus gathering when blood was about to be spilt.

Reality snapped back violently.

Aza gasped as consciousness hit him like a tidal wave. His body collapsed onto the floor, shaking.

The chanting stopped.

Yhesus3 and the priest stood still, their silence thick with finality. Only the little boy continued, his hands striking the gong in a frenzied rhythm, lost in madness.

The Yhesus priest stepped forward. Without a word, he took Aza's hand and pressed his thumb against the Yhesus death seal.

The ritual was complete. The mark had been made.

Aza lay there, unmoving.

An hour passed, maybe more.

His mind spun with questions.

What was the seal for? Who did I just kill?

His thoughts blurred, his body shutting down. A deep force overtook him, his consciousness slipping into the void.

But he wasn't dead—not yet.

Footsteps echoed around him.

Why does death keep running from me?

A shadow loomed above him. Familiar. Heavy with malice.

"You want all the power and all your desires, you ungrateful fool," Yhesus3 echoed.

The voice thundered in his mind.

Aza saw the shadow clearly now. He had seen it before. At the club. A few weeks before the campaign.

What did Yhesus do to me? What have they done to my mother?

He fought to wake up, to pull himself back into reality. But the more the gong played, the harder it became. His body refused to move. His soul felt trapped.

Is this about the ghost? My unknown son? Jealousy? Have I become a threat?

Then—

A crushing force clamped around his neck.

His body convulsed, gasping for air. The pressure tightened. And then, he saw her.

His mother's face. Unstable. Fading. Disappearing into the shadows.

Aza jolted awake.

His chest heaved. His neck ached from the grip.

The room was empty—just flickering candles.

Beside him, lying still and lifeless, was Adamu, his driver.

Aza sat up slowly, struggling for breath. The phantom grip on his neck lingered, as if something—or someone—had almost dragged him beyond the threshold.

Moonlight streamed through the windows, casting long shadows across the room.

Aza bent over, reaching for his driver's wristwatch.

It was two o'clock in the morning.

How long have I been here?

His breath hitched.

They had left him there to die.

There was no way out of the shrine unless the priest or Yhesus3 returned. And if they didn't, it meant only one thing—they had failed.

A slow, seething rage bubbled inside him.

It consumed every rational thought, every lingering doubt. Even the voices—the ones that always whispered in the back of his mind—had gone silent.

What remained was an emptiness so profound it felt euphoric, as if he had died and come back to life.

The first ritual had made him a Yhesus.

But whatever had just happened?

It had made him the devil.

Aza clenched his fists.

With immense effort, he crawled out of the position he had been trapped in since morning. Whoever wanted him dead would come for his body at dawn.

He needed to get out.

His legs still refused to move, and he had no phone. He leaned over his driver, checking his pockets for one.

Nothing.

He hissed in disappointment.

Aza dragged himself towards the door, inch by painful inch, until he reached the wall and slumped against it.

His body screamed for rest, but his mind refused to stop.

Then, a flash—Reana, his daughter.

She had called that morning, excited. School was out for the term, and he had promised to pick her up.

Aza squeezed his eyes shut.

Shame cut through him.

He had failed her.

Just as he had failed his mother.

Every time she waited for me, I gave her reasons not to. Every time she needed me, I was never there.

No wonder she despised him. No wonder she treated him like a stranger.

And he couldn't blame her.

He had promised his mother he would be a good father.

Now she was gone.

And he had failed.

The shrine tent had six compartments, with two inner rooms accessible only to the priest.

Before reaching them, one had to pass through two circular corridors, flanked by two compartments on each side. From above, the entire structure resembled the face of a bull.

Aza had never explored each compartment in full, but to keep himself awake that night, he decided to crawl through them—one by one.

The corridors were built with brick, reminiscent of a Buddhist shrine, their dim lighting barely illuminated by the moonlight filtering through the roof.

There was no electricity here—only the flickering glow of candlelight.

As Aza moved through the passage, he noticed how

the corridor seemed to constrict, forcing him into a curled position.

The farther he went, the narrower it became.

Emerging into the first chamber, his eyes adjusted to the eerie sight—a skeletal structure resembling a cow's spine stretched across the room.

Candles flickered in each corner, casting long, shifting shadows over the walls, which were covered in unsettling art.

Beautiful, yet undeniably sinister.

A fine white powder had been sprinkled in patterns along the floor, tracing the edges of the walls and leading towards the next doorway.

Each compartment was shaped more like a passageway than a room—narrow, elongated, suffocating.

When Aza reached the third room, recognition struck him like a blow.

The priest's chamber.

The place of his first bloodbath.

The submerged corridors.

The animal bones.

He remembered them all too well.

That day was burned into his memory.

The metallic taste of blood rose unbidden in his mind, lingering like a ghost.

Aza slumped into a dark corner, exhaustion seeping into his bones.

His head drooped.

And before he realised it—he had drifted off.

A sound jolted him awake.

His body tensed.

He felt... different.

Stronger.

The room was still bathed in darkness, save for the golden candlelight from the first chamber and a faint blue glow from the corridors.

Heart pounding, he crawled back towards the entrance, ears straining.

Footsteps.

Soft.

Deliberate.

Someone was leaving the corridor.

"Did they not see me? Or did they think I was already dead?" He muttered.

Panic surged through him.

If it was the one who wanted him dead, they were coming to retrieve his corpse.

He needed a weapon.

Frantically, his eyes swept the room—

Bones.

Artworks.

Lanterns.

Nothing he could use.

"Hello, where is Aza's body?"

Yhesus3 was on the phone with the priest.

"Right there," the priest replied. "I left it beside the driver's."

"I can't find him. Did someone take him away?"

"No one has the keys. Was the door broken?" the priest asked.

"No."

Yhesus3's voice was tense.

"Do you think he's still alive?"

Silence.

Then—

"No, that's impossible," the priest replied, his tone suddenly fearful. "His soul is gone. He can't be alive."

Yhesus3 cursed under his breath and ended the call.

He moved to the other side of the building, scanning the shadows.

Minutes later, he lit his torch and approached the second compartment.

Inside, Aza's heart pounded violently.

He gripped a lantern in one hand and an animal femur from the room's decorations in the other.

The footsteps quickened, growing louder.

He could see Yhesus3's shadow flickering against the walls.

It was him.

He wanted Aza dead.

He had stepped on his neck, trying to kill him spiritually.

But somehow, his mother had saved him.

Adrenaline surged through Aza's veins.

Yhesus3 noticed the faint glow coming from the corridor.

He exhaled sharply, his voice cold. "So, you're still alive." He chuckled. "How bold of you. Why don't you come out and show yourself?"

Aza didn't move.

He needed him closer.

Yhesus3 stepped forward, his gaze sweeping the dimly lit room.

When his eyes landed on Aza's motionless limbs, a smirk crossed his face.

"You already look dead," he sneered. "Why not do yourself a favor?"

Aza thought, You can say that again, but not today.

The moment Yhesus3 leaned in, Aza hurled the lantern at him, the loosened fuel tank spilling its contents.

The flames erupted instantly.

Yhesus3 screamed as fire engulfed his face, his phone slipping from his grasp.

Aza seized the opportunity.

Using the bone for leverage, he dragged himself forward and pulled the phone towards him.

Yhesus3, blinded by pain, tried to crawl towards the door.

But Aza wasn't done.

With one last push, he knocked him back onto the floor and watched as the flames consumed him.

For a long moment, only the crackling of fire filled the air

When Aza was sure he was dead, he turned his attention to the phone.

Aza dialled Becky's number and gave her an address to pick him up.

He knew he had to get out of the shrine before someone else came looking for Yhesus3.

He tried to stand but couldn't.

His legs refused him.

He had to be fast.

The shrine was nearly a mile from the main road, and morning was fast approaching.

He started dragging himself forward, ignoring the sharp pain shooting through his body.

Half an hour later, he was still in the woods, but the road was finally in sight.

His phone rang. Becky.

He answered.

"I'll be there soon."

He forced himself to move faster, the smell of his own burnt flesh upsetting his stomach.

Every nerve in his body screamed, but he didn't care.

He just needed to get out.

At last, Aza reached the roadside and collapsed, taking a few seconds to catch his breath.

For the first time in hours, he felt something close to relief.

He was alive.

The sky was beginning to lighten.

He pushed forward until he saw the white Nissan parked in front of the mechanic shop he had described to Becky.

But as he got closer, his stomach twisted.

Becky wasn't there.

Instead, his former driver—now Becky's driver—stood beside the car.

The moment the driver spotted him, he ran over.

"Oga, what happened?!" he shouted, rushing to help Aza to his feet.

Aza barely registered the words.

The moment the driver's hands steadied him, the weight of his injuries hit him all at once—

The pain.

The exhaustion.

The grief he had pushed aside.

And then, the thought crept in.

Was his mother dead?

He tried to shove it away.

But it clung to him like a shadow.

Reana sat on the front porch, watching her father's second wife—Becky—feed the babies outside the guest house.

Pathetic.

Her father had gotten another woman pregnant while her mother was in the UK.

How stupid could he be?

She had no interest in forming a relationship with Becky. Anything her father did wasn't her concern—just like she was never his concern.

Tired of the sight, Reana got up and went inside.

As she walked through the hallway, childhood memories flooded back—the strange noises from her father's room, the heavy, unspoken sadness in the house.

Her mother was never the comforting type, either.

Life had been cold from the very start.

"Maybe I should go to my aunt's place for a while," she said to herself.

She made up her mind, packed her bags, and headed out.

At the main door, she paused.

The security guard stood by the open gate as a white Nissan drove in.

She frowned.

Her father didn't own a white Nissan.

Curious, she stayed put, waiting to see who would step out.

The car pulled up to the front porch, stopping just a few feet from where she stood.

Aza saw her through the windshield.

His heart dropped.

What will she think? How will she react?

He hesitated until the driver stepped out.

Reana's eyes narrowed.

She didn't recognise the car or understand why her father wasn't coming out.

Then the driver hurried to the passenger side, opened the door, and helped Aza out.

Reana's expression shifted from disdain to confusion.

Becky was in shock. She ran to meet him.

"Aza! Are you coming from the hospital? Where's your driver? Where's your car?" Her voice was sharp, frantic.

Aza couldn't answer.

The weight of everything crushed him.

Reana stood motionless, still staring.

Becky and the driver helped Aza inside and lowered him onto the couch.

The silence in the room was heavy. Too heavy.

Reana stepped closer to Aza, her arms folded.

"What happened to you?"

Aza exhaled.

"It's a long story, my dear."

Silence hung between them for a moment.

Then, trying to shift the tension, Aza asked, "How was school?"

Reana's eyes darkened.

"Fine. Now tell me what happened to you."

This time, her voice was sharper, laced with anger.

"I had an accident."

Becky and the driver stood nearby, exchanging uneasy glances.

"Please, leave us," Aza said.

The driver quietly stepped away, but Becky remained.

"And you too."

Becky blinked.

"Me?"

"Yes, you."

Before Becky could protest, a piercing wail echoed from outside, growing closer.

Reana turned towards the door.

"Who is that?"

She rushed forward just as a familiar voice cried out:

"Aunty!"

Reana froze.

"What is it?"

The words that followed shattered the air.

"Mama is dead!"

"What?!" Reana's voice cracked. "How?!"

Aza felt the world tilt.

His body, already weakened, went completely numb.

His sister burst into the room and collapsed in front of him, sobbing uncontrollably.

She grabbed his shirt with trembling hands.

"Brother, what happened to Mama? Say something!"

Aza could only watch as Reana broke down, her screams tearing through the silence.

"What killed Mama?! And why didn't anyone tell me my father was paralyzed?!" Reana asked, sobbing.

She was totally confused.

Aza's sister snapped her head up, her face twisting in shock.

"What?"

Wiping her tears, she turned to him.

"You were in an accident? When? How?"

Reana looked at Becky, demanding answers.

"You knew, didn't you?"

Becky shook her head.

"I just found out today too. I saw him lying on the ground this morning and told him to go to the hospital."

A heart-wrenching cry escaped from Aza's sister.

She clutched her chest.

"Brother, what happened to you?" She sobbed deeply.

Before anyone could speak, Reana spun around and bolted outside.

Aza tried to call after her, but his voice failed him.

Liverpool, England

"Hello? What are you saying?"

"Dad is paralyzed... and Grandma is dead," Reana said over the phone, holding back tears.

Ann gasped. "My God!" she shouted.

Nioma, startled, looked up from her plate. "Mum, what is it?"

Ann forced a smile. "Go back to your food."

Her voice wavered as she turned her attention back to the phone. "Where are you now?"

"I'm at the house with Dad. Did you know he has children with another woman?"

There was a pause before her mother answered.

"Yes. Go to your aunt's house now."

"What?!" Reana's voice rose in disbelief. "You knew?"

"Yes, I was informed, but I don't care. He can do whatever he wants."

Ann's words hit like a slap.

"Mum, you want me to leave Dad alone in this state?"

"He's not alone," Ann said coolly. "He has a wife and kids, remember?"

"But Mum—"

"No buts. Do as I say and call me when you get there."

The line went dead.

Ann clutched her stomach as she slid down beside the kitchen counter, her body trembling. The weight of the conversation pressed against her chest.

"The only woman who had my back in this dead marriage is gone. There's nothing left for me to go back to," she whispered.

Hearing about Aza living with another woman and their children stung, but deep down, she knew it was a good excuse to go through with the divorce.

Aza sat in the centre, surrounded by men.

The air was thick with tension.

Opposite him, the priest stood, unmoving.

Locking eyes with the priest, Aza spoke with quiet intensity. "Before you kill me, know this—I will kill you first."

The priest studied him, then smiled.

"The two men who wanted you dead are gone. You have nothing to fear."

Aza's eyes narrowed. "Who was the second?"

"The driver assigned to you by Yhesus."

Aza frowned. "He wasn't assigned to me by Yhesus."

"He was. You just didn't know."

Aza let out a slow breath.

Even under oath, there were no brothers.

At that moment, Aza realised he would never chase political office again.

He had gained something far greater—the ultimate power.

He was now at the top rank of the Yhesus cult. With this, he could control anyone and take whatever he desired.

IMPUNITY

6

Adonis walked towards a girl sitting alone by the window in the classroom.

"Hello."

She turned, looked at him briefly, then shifted her gaze back to the window.

Undeterred, he approached with a smile. "Hi there."

This time, she responded. "Hello."

"Are you done with your classes?"

She turned to face him. "Yes, I am."

"I'm Adonis," he said with a smile.

"Good."

He hesitated, then asked, "What's your name?"

"Why are you asking?" Reana snapped, staring him in the face. Irritated, she picked up her bag and made to leave.

"Nothing serious, just trying to get to know you," he said quickly, stopping her in her tracks. "So… what exams are you preparing for?"

She shot him an unimpressed look. "Dude, why are you interrogating me?"

Adonis raised his hands in surrender. "Didn't mean to sound like that. I just saw you sitting alone and thought I'd say hi."

"Is sitting alone a problem here?"

"No, no," he said quickly

She turned back to the window, uninterested.

Adonis lingered for a moment, scrolling through his phone.

"Adonis!" Felix's voice rang from the doorway. "What's up? We need to go."

Adonis got to his feet. "Oh, okay. I'll see you some other time."

She didn't turn or reply.

As they stepped out, Felix smirked. "What were you doing there?"

"Trying to say hello."

"Do you know her?" Felix asked. He glanced at Reana, then back at Adonis. "So how did it go?"

"Not really. I've seen her around a couple of times."

Felix chuckled. "So you're trying to toast her? Isn't she too young for you? I bet she's like fifteen or sixteen."

"Nah, she looks older than that." He looked back at Reana as though he could confirm her age just by staring.

Felix laughed. "Rich man's child. Of course, she looks big." He patted Adonis on the shoulder. "They grow like agric fowl."

Adonis raised a brow. "And you know this how, CNN?"

"Haven't you seen the car that drops her off? Bro, you just come to this tutorial centre dulling. You don't even know what's happening."

Adonis shrugged. "How would I know? I'm not a newsagent."

"Fool! No one is a newsagent. We just observe, you goat."

Adonis laughed. "Well, I haven't seen her come in before, so—"

Felix waved a hand dismissively. "You wouldn't want to

mess with that kind of girl anyway. She's probably a spoiled brat." He paused. "Haven't you seen the way she separates herself from the rest of the class? Like we're not on her level."

"That's what you think. Not all rich kids are spoiled."

"Not all, but all rich girls are."

"Not all," Adonis insisted.

Felix smirked. "Of course, you'd say that—anything to get in her pants."

Adonis scoffed. "I'm not even trying to. Why do you always talk foolishly? Does it run in your family?"

Felix's grin disappeared. "Say that one more time, and if I don't slap the shit out of you—"

"Chill, I was just joking."

Felix rolled his eyes. Then, suddenly, he pointed. "Why is that teacher standing at the security post like he's lost the will to live?"

One of their teachers, in an undersized trouser that barely reached his ankles, stood at the security post staring into nothing. His wrinkled shirt billowed in the wind, and at intervals, he scratched his head in confusion.

Felix pointed to him.

Adonis glanced over. "What?"

They both burst into laughter.

As they left the tutorial centre, Felix stretched and groaned. "I can't wait for these Joint Admission Matriculation Board exams to be over. I need to cruise this town."

Adonis smirked. "Just say you want to become a G-boy and forget school."

Felix laughed. "Look at you, someone who doesn't even have a sponsor for school talking. If I do G, at least I can pay your school fees. When you graduate, you can work for me. How about that?"

Adonis frowned. "Is that supposed to be a joke? Because it wasn't funny."

Felix sighed. "Relax, you take things too seriously."

"You actually sound dumb sometimes."

"Oh, but what you said about me earlier wasn't dumb? Taxi!" Felix called out, flagging down a cab. "Street beside Saro Wiwa Polytechnic," he told the driver as they got in.

A few minutes into the ride, Adonis muttered, "You know, I don't actually have anyone to put me through school. That wasn't a joke to me."

Felix nudged him. "You could always ask your new lover for help." He grinned. "Kidding!"

Adonis sighed. "Not funny."

Felix's tone softened. "Relax, things will work out. Even if you don't go now, you can later. Just keep hustling and learning. Building and construction isn't child's play—it'll pay off. Look at me, I don't even want to go to school and I have sponsors. Maybe you can go in my name and hand me the certificate when you're done. What do you think?"

Adonis burst out laughing. "How do you say that with a straight face?"

Felix grinned. "At least I tried. Driver, ahn ahn, why are you changing lanes?"

"I need to buy fuel," the driver replied.

Felix groaned. "These drivers are something else. Why would you carry passengers without fueling first?"

"Una sorry o. No vex for me."

Adonis glanced at Felix. "Are you heading home?"

"Nope."

"Where to?"

"I'll chill with my guys for a while. It's just 4 PM What would I be doing at home?"

"I'm heading to the workshop."

"Oh, okay. Ronaldo or Messi?"

Adonis smirked. "Messi, of course. Are you blind?"

"No, you're the one who's blind. Ronaldo is the most awarded for a reason."

"Awards don't equal greatness on the field. Plus, Messi is La Liga's all-time top scorer."

Felix shook his head. "Yeah, but Ronaldo has the most official goals in history. He's the G.O.A.T. I don't even know why I argue with you."

Adonis sighed. "Whatever. None of them are putting money in my pocket."

He leaned back, staring out the window.

The conversation with Felix had distracted him, but the weight of his struggles crept back in. Memories of failing the Joint Admissions and Matriculation Board (JAMB) exam and his mother dragging him to this tutorial centre stung.

Since the exam was necessary to get into a tertiary institution, he needed to excel in it.

He was good at drawing and painting, but just an average student overall.

He knew gaining experience at Mr Ero's furniture and construction company could help him transition into architecture—if he passed JAMB and found the funds to further his education.

"Like Felix said, things will work out," he muttered to himself.

As the cab approached Dunamis Shop, near the bend before Tantalizers Plaza, Adonis sat up.

"Stop here, driver," he said.

Adonis smirked. "See you tomorrow?"

Felix raised a brow. "Adonis, there are no lectures

tomorrow."

Adonis laughed. "Ah, I totally forgot."

"Get that rich girl off your mind and you'll be just fine," Felix teased.

Adonis rolled his eyes. "Felix, stop being stupid."

They both burst into laughter as Adonis hopped out of the cab.

When Adonis arrived at the workshop, he slipped into his usual overalls and was about to start sanding a wooden dining table when he heard the familiar sound of his boss's black Golf Metro pulling up.

Despite owning a sleek black Honda Civic, Mr Ero preferred the Golf—it was more practical for transporting tools and workers.

Mr Eroboghene had built a solid reputation in the industry. With years of experience under his belt, his extensive knowledge and hands-on expertise set him apart.

Interestingly, he had neither a university degree nor a senior school certificate. Instead, he had gained valuable experience working at a construction firm overseas before returning to Nigeria to establish his now-thriving business.

For him, the work was more than just a means to earn a living—it was a passion. Anyone who worked with him could see and feel it. He made it look effortless, but in reality, the craft demanded creativity and precision.

It was no surprise that Mr Ero had taken Adonis under his wing. Adonis's exceptional drawing and painting skills had earned him a position at the workshop—not as an apprentice, but as an employee. His talent extended beyond paper to furniture and brickwork, giving his projects a distinctive flair.

In addition to assigning him house remodelling tasks, Mr Ero personally mentored him in furniture-making, welding, tiling, and interior design.

Mr Ero placed a large Arch D blueprint on the drawing table. "Drop what you're doing and came," he instructed.

Adonis suppressed a smile at his boss's usual grammatical errors but knew better than to laugh.

"Okay, sir," he responded, stepping forward.

"This were supposed to be a duplex in a Government Residential Area, but the project were abandoned before completion," Mr Ero explained, pointing at the original floor plan. "I needed you to add some spice to it."

Adonis knew that when Mr Ero said "add spice," he meant a complete redesign.

"This is huge. I've never worked on a duplex before, but I can give it a shot, sir," Adonis said, studying the blueprint.

"There are nothing you can't do, my boy," Mr Ero assured him.

"Thank you, sir."

"Before you thank me, take a look at the current state." Mr Ero pulled out his heavy Samsung notepad and scrolled through a series of pictures and videos.

Adonis peered at the screen. "Wow, that's a lot of damage," he muttered.

Mr Ero nodded. "Here's the interior. Now, give me an rundown of how you go approach the work."

"Sir, I need time to study it properly."

"I'll gave you 15 minutes. I'll be back," Mr Ero said before stepping out.

Left alone, Adonis examined the images more closely.

He quickly noted several issues—the duplex lacked proper ventilation, the architectural design was outdated, and the entrance porch was disproportionately small for a building of its size. The roofing was also obsolete, and the walls appeared to have been painted without proper screeding.

Before he could finish his assessment, Mr Ero returned. "Adonis, wetin you have for me?"

"Sir, I've identified a few key areas that need improvement. The built-in cabinetry, doors, windows, ceilings, arches, and columns all need remodeling. However, the interior is spacious and bright enough, so a fresh coat of paint should suffice."

"Good," Mr Ero said. "I wan see your redesign. How long will it take?"

"Because of my JAMB tutorials, I'll need about two weeks," Adonis replied.

"Okay, but I might need it sooner. No make me lose money," Mr Ero warned.

"Understood, sir."

Although Mr Ero knew he would eventually need a full team for the project, he valued Adonis's input. He admired how the young man thrived under pressure and wanted to hear his perspective before consulting a certified architect.

Adonis had come a long way—his problem-solving skills had sharpened considerably, and his creative instincts had grown stronger. This project would be a challenge, but he was ready to take it on.

At 7:30 PM, Adonis was putting the finishing touches on the wooden dining set he had been painting all day. He regretted using spray paint—it had taken longer than he expected. Worse still, some primed areas weren't properly coated, forcing him to repeat the process.

He checked his watch again. He couldn't afford to miss the last bus to Wimpay.

By 8:00 PM, he finally packed up and left for the park, feeling both exhausted and accomplished.

Balancing JAMB tutorial classes with construction work was no joke.

Sitting in the back of the bus, Adonis watched a little boy argue with his mother over his hairstyle. He absentmindedly ran his fingers over his own weaved-back hair, wondering if his mother—whom he had never met—would have approved. *Maybe she would think I was cute... or maybe not.* He sighed.

Auntie is great. She's always been my mother.

Suddenly, the bus slowed down.

"Shit! I was trying to avoid this traffic," Adonis groaned.

"It's probably the police," the lady beside him muttered.

"Why do they always set up their checkpoints near bad roads?"

"So you don't try to run, I guess," she replied.

"Run from what? So now we all have to be stuck here because of them?"

"If they're actually checking for anything serious, sure. But they're mostly here to extort drivers."

"Exactly! And the funny thing is, they wouldn't even notice if an armed robber drove right past them."

"They'd probably just collect money and let him rob in peace," she said, rolling her eyes.

They both laughed, but the situation wasn't funny. It was frustrating.

As they approached the checkpoint, Adonis noticed all public transport drivers being handed numbered slips.

"What's the number for?" he asked the lady.

"No idea," she shrugged.

"Hey! Search that bus!" a police officer shouted from the rear, signalling his colleagues.

"Hey! Stop!" another officer barked, jumping in front of the bus to force it to a halt.

"What is it now?" Adonis muttered under his breath.

A policeman with tired, heavy eyes yanked the door open

and swept his flashlight over the passengers. The moment his beam landed on the little boy with red-tinted hair, his expression darkened.

"You! Step down!" he commanded.

"Please, he's my son," the mother protested.

"Madam, I'm not talking to you. Oga, I said step down!"

Adonis sighed. "He is a young boy. Or is it because of what he did to his hair? So you can't even dye your hair in this country?"

"I wonder," the lady beside him murmured. "They now assume anyone with colored hair is a criminal."

Another officer sneered. "Madam, you let your son carry this kind of hair, and you're still defending him?"

"I'm not! I've told him to change it," the mother argued.

"So, you don't listen to your parents, abi? Are you a cultist? A fraudster?"

The boy shook his head in disapproval. He was trembling, too scared to speak.

A passenger at the back groaned. "What is the meaning of all this?"

"Who said that?" an officer snapped, scanning the bus again.

"Oga police, leave the boy alone. Kids dye their hair these days. What's the big deal? We just want to go home," another passenger said.

"You want to teach me my job? Do you want me to bring you down too?"

"For what?" a third passenger challenged.

Another policeman pointed at Adonis. "Look at this one—hair weaved back. Another cultist! Oya, bring him down!"

Adonis froze, pretending as though he had no idea he was being called out.

"Oga, are you deaf?" the officer snapped. "Come down!"

"I no hear wetin you talk, you no talk am loud," Adonis replied dryly.

The officer's eyes flashed with anger. "So, you want make me dey shout, abi?"

Adonis sighed and stepped down from the bus. The passengers started murmuring in protest.

"Oga, who are you? Why did you weave your hair? You be cultist?" another officer demanded.

"How does weaving my hair make me a cultist?" Adonis shot back.

"You dey question me?"

A burly officer stepped forward, slapping him, he grabbed Adonis by the belt. "You think you're smart, abi? You go be scapegoat tonight."

He signalled to the others to let the boy with tinted hair go.

The driver got off the bus. "Ah ah, where una dey take am go? He never do anything!"

"Do you want to join him?" an officer threatened.

"No, but I know him. He's not a bad person."

Passengers grumbled as they got off, unwilling to continue their journey without their driver. But the man ignored them, following the officers as they dragged Adonis to their post.

They searched his backpack.

"Oga, come see," one of them called. "Na building plans full the laptop."

The head officer frowned. "You be architect?"

"I'm a student," Adonis replied.

"When you talk to me, you say sir! Understand?"

Silence.

The driver nudged him. "Answer now."

"Yes, sir," Adonis muttered.

"Where you dey school wey dem allow you carry hair like this?"

"I'm preparing for JAMB and learning architecture, sir."

"You never even enter university, you don dey raise shoulder," one officer, skinny and tall, said.

"You too old to be writing JAMB. How old you be?" Another officer, who seemed to be the highest-ranking among them, asked.

Adonis clenched his jaw. "Twenty."

"Who buy this laptop for you?"

He was already exhausted from the questions.

His boss had warned him never to take the laptop outside work, but he sometimes needed it for urgent tasks. If he said his boss, they might call him. If he said his parents, they might ask to call them too.

"My parents," he lied.

"Where dem dey work?"

"My mum is a trader, and my—"

"Abeg, carry your laptop dey go," the head officer interrupted, uninterested.

"Ah ah, oga, no be so!" another officer protested. "He must drop something!"

The officer hesitated, then turned to Adonis. "I'm letting you go because of this driver. Next time you talk back, you go sleep for cell. You hear me?"

"Yes, sir," Adonis muttered.

The officer then turned to the driver. "Oga driver, since na you talk for am, you go drop something for us."

"Ah! E no be my boy o, just my regular passenger. And una don make me lose all my customers tonight," the driver complained.

"Oga driver, drop something. You no work yesterday?"

Sighing, the driver pulled out a crumpled ₦500 note.

The officer scoffed. "Five hundred?"

"Oga officer, abeg manage am. Na wetin I get."

The head officer nodded, and his subordinate collected the money.

Adonis exhaled, trailing the driver as they both headed for the bus.

"So, these passengers just left their money and took another bus?" Adonis asked as he settled into the passenger seat, adjusting his bag.

"Small oga, you go dey careful with these policemen o," the driver warned.

"They can go to hell. Rubbish," Adonis snapped, still fuming.

"Nor be by rubbish o. Dem fit mistakenly shoot you, and **NOTHING GO HAPPEN**. Na because I know you, I follow you," the driver said, shaking his head.

"Thank you, boss man."

"Na so dem carry my brother last month for this same road. We go bail am for cell because he carry dreadlocks. Dem say him be Yahoo boy. Even talk say dem see white woman for him phone. My brother swear say white woman no dey him phone."

"Seriously?" Adonis asked, eyebrows raised.

"Yes o," the driver sighed.

"These men are really sick. What is this country turning into?" Adonis muttered, rubbing his temple.

The rest of the trip was silent. He had always heard stories of police harassment, but he thought people exaggerated. Now, having experienced it firsthand, he was shaken.

How could this be normal? Why wasn't anyone doing anything about it? He couldn't wait for the day the youth would revolt against the police force. That day would be interesting.

"Harassing young boys just because they want to extort them," he mumbled, still in disbelief. He decided not to tell his parents. His mum would probably curse him out over his hair instead of condemning the police. Better to brush it off like he usually did.

For a brief moment, he considered taking out his braids, but he dismissed the thought.

"No one will bully me into cutting my hair. Except I want to," he murmured. "The police can choke on their shit."

He wondered if mentioning his parents' status would have made a difference—would they have let him go, or would they have demanded more money? The thought infuriated him.

"Why are you coming home this late? Adonis, you know this area is not safe at night," Aunty Annetta said the moment he stepped inside.

"I know. My bus broke down, so I had to wait before getting another one," he replied, offering a less dramatic explanation.

He walked straight to the kitchen, his body drained. The slap from the officers still echoed in his head, leaving him dizzy. He could barely see straight.

"Damn, those officers are wicked," he muttered under his breath as he grabbed some semo and egusi soup. He had just settled at the kitchen table when a knock came at the door.

That should be Dad.

He closed his eyes for a second, praying his uncle wasn't drunk again. To this day, he couldn't understand how his aunt coped with a man who was barely sober. Their marriage felt like a bone stuck in someone's throat—something either of them could swallow or spit out.

Their lack of children only made matters worse.

Adonis had always been a part of their home, but his roots ran deeper. He was the son of Annetta's older sister, Karisha, who had died during childbirth.

Annetta had taken him in, raising him as her own. Karisha had never revealed the identity of his father, and Annetta never pushed.

When Adonis turned eighteen, she finally told him about his biological mother and how she had died. But to him, it made no difference—Annetta was the only mother he had ever known.

As for his father, he never asked. Annetta had already told him she had no information.

He had watched his aunt struggle—going from doctor to doctor, church to church, searching for a child of her own. Her husband had been supportive in his own way, but his drinking always got the best of him.

And tonight, Adonis wasn't sure if he had the energy to deal with it.

"I'm coming," Adonis called out as he made his way to the door.

The moment he opened it, a drunken Pere collapsed onto him, the stench of beer and spirits thick on his clothes.

"Dad, why now? Why are you doing this?" Adonis sighed, struggling to steady him before guiding him to the nearest chair.

He didn't bother calling for Annetta. She was probably already aware her husband had returned but, as usual, chose to stay out of sight, like she always did whenever he came home late—and drunk.

Adonis didn't mind. He had cleaned Pere up more times than he could count. But tonight, the man was out cold, already snoring before Adonis could do anything.

As he reached to take off his father's shoes and loosen his clothes, he noticed Annetta standing quietly by the corridor leading to the bedroom.

"Leave him alone. Have you eaten yet?" she asked.

"No, Mum. Don't worry, I'll just take his clothes off so he can rest properly," Adonis replied, his voice hesitant.

"Adonis, please leave him alone. Go and eat your food."

"No, Mum, I can't leave him like this," he whispered.

"I said leave him."

Her tone left no room for argument. He swallowed his protest, rising slowly from his father's side before heading to the kitchen. As he glanced back, he saw Annetta turn and retreat into her room.

Sitting at the table, he stared at his meal, his appetite gone. Just moments ago, he had looked forward to eating, but now his taste buds felt numb.

He wished Annetta didn't have to go through all this. She was the kindest woman he had ever known. Sometimes, he wondered—if his mother had been alive, would she have been this kind too?

The next morning, Adonis started his usual Saturday jog just before the sun would wake.

Most weekends, he would stop by Damiete's or Felix's houses so they could run together, but today, he hesitated. He didn't want to slip up and mention his run-in with the police the night before.

After a moment of deliberation, he decided to call only Damiete.

As he approached Damiete's house, he spotted him already jogging out.

"Hey, guy, what's up?" Damiete said, raising his hand for

a high five.

"I'm good," Adonis replied, slapping his palm. "What about you?"

"Just some woman trouble here and there, nothing serious."

"I wasn't expecting much," Adonis said with a smirk.

"Clown. Where's Felix? He's not running today?"

"I don't know. I knocked on his gate—no response," Adonis said.

"This morning?"

"No, last night while I was running," Adonis replied.

"You run at night?" Damiete asked, raising a brow.

"My God, Damiete! This morning, of course," Adonis snapped.

"I don't get you."

"You know what? Never mind. Speaking of last night, I got stopped by the police."

"Oh… let me guess. Your hair?"

"What's wrong with a guy weaving his hair?"

"You forget we live in a fucking third-world country. But I hope they didn't harass you too much?" Damiete asked.

"Guy, they slapped me and went through my laptop."

"They checked your computer? That's a breach of privacy. Do they even know they need a search warrant for that?"

"Search warrant ko, search warrant ni. Forget those guys," Adonis muttered.

"Wow, what a night. But at least it wasn't worse… So, how was the slap, though?" Damiete asked with a smirk.

"What's funny? You and Felix joke about everything," Adonis scoffed.

Just then, a tricycle pulled up beside them.

"Speak of the devil," Adonis muttered.

"Who's the devil?" Felix asked, stepping out and

immediately grabbing Adonis by the collar. "You bitches were talking about me, right?"

"Chill, yo," Adonis said, laughing.

"You wanna beat him up? He just took a slap last night from the police. Have mercy on him, brother," Damiete said, chuckling.

"What? How? Why?" Felix asked, letting go of Adonis' shirt.

"I didn't know you had such loose lips. You're a real bitch," Adonis said, shooting a glare at Damiete.

"Dude got slapped by the police because of his hair," Damiete said, now laughing even harder. "He wants to be a gangster so bad."

"Bro, your hair isn't even long enough to be braiding it," Felix chimed in. "And last time, you were complaining about how tight it was. Now you got slapped for the same braids? Hahaha!"

"I can't believe you two are laughing about my traumatic experience. It's all fun and jokes until it's your turn," Adonis muttered.

"Guy, don't curse us now, it's just jokes," Damiete said, still grinning.

"Yeah, that's what I said," Adonis replied dryly.

"Okay, okay. What really happened?" Felix asked, finally serious.

"Now you want to know?" Adonis scoffed. "Anyway, that's what happened."

"Mehn, these police officers are getting out of hand in these streets," Felix muttered, shaking his head.

They had been jogging for over 45 minutes when Damiete suggested they stop for some chilled water. They paused at a roadside shop.

"Are you guys going to Osaretin's birthday party?" Damiete asked as he took a sip from his bottle.

"Of course," Felix replied. "Who would miss that?"

"I heard it's at a club," Damiete added.

"Really? I thought it was at his house," Adonis said, surprised.

"Nope, West End Club," Damiete clarified.

"Cool," Adonis nodded.

"You're coming, right?" Damiete asked, looking at him.

"Of course, he's coming. Why are you even asking?" Felix cut in.

"I guess you're my spokesperson now," Adonis said, rolling his eyes.

Just then, Damiete's phone rang. He glanced at the screen. "Guys, my mum is calling. I gotta go. See you at the party tonight." Without waiting for a response, he flagged down a tricycle and hopped in, heading towards East Avenue.

"I should get going too," Adonis said, stretching. "I need to do some laundry."

"Alright, I'll see you at the party," Felix said, shaking his hand.

"Yeah," Adonis replied.

"I'm heading to the phone shop first," Felix added before walking off.

Adonis resumed jogging back home.

Around 7:00 PM, as Adonis was in the kitchen, Annetta called out from the living room.

"Are you still going to your friend's birthday party?"

"Yeah," he answered, rinsing his hands.

"You should get going before it gets too dark."

"Mum, if I leave now, I'll be the first to arrive. Don't worry, I'll head out by 7:30."

When he first mentioned the party earlier that day, Annetta had hesitated about letting him go. But as always, doing her laundry worked like a charm.

"I'm going for fellowship," she said, picking up her bag. "You're spending the night there, right?"

"Yes, Mum."

"Alright then. Make sure you come back early so you can prepare for service."

"Yes, Mum," Adonis said, drying his hands.

With that, she left, and he went to get ready for the night ahead.

"Man, that party was lit," Felix said, stretching his arms. "But the girls? Meh."

"They were alright," Adonis replied. "You're always worried about girls."

"What else am I here for?" Felix smirked.

"Ask Nimi, that's not on me," Osaretin shrugged.

Felix didn't waste a second. "Hey, Nimi!" he called out.

Damiete shook his head. "You're really going to ask her? Are you that desperate?"

Nimi walked up to them, grinning. "Hey boys. Birthday boy. I know you all had fun."

"We did," Felix said. "Except for the girls. They were dulling."

Nimi chuckled. "Yeah, I noticed. My girls were at another birthday party. They would've shut things down."

Felix's face lit up. "Where are they? We can take this party there!"

"Yesss!" Osaretin agreed.

"Redington Hotel, not far from here," Nimi replied.

"Say less." Felix turned to Osaretin. "You're driving, right?"

"Of course," Osaretin said.

They piled into one of Osaretin's father's cars, parked outside the club. The road was quiet—it was past 11 PM, and traffic had thinned.

Osaretin glanced at Nimi, who was in the passenger seat. "How many of your friends are there?"

"Five, I think."

"Perfect. One per person," he grinned.

"Haha, are you picking them like groceries?" Nimi teased.

"Just to hang out, have fun. Birthday boy gets first pick."

Felix scoffed. "Hold up, why do you get first pick? I made the suggestion!"

"Come on, man," Damiete said. "Let him breathe, geez."

As they neared the main road, Felix frowned. "This road is bad. We should take the other route."

"But there are always police officers there," Adonis warned.

"It's late. I doubt they'll be around," Damiete reasoned.

The moment they turned onto the main road, their hearts sank. A roadblock. Two cars ahead.

"Are those police?" Adonis asked, shifting in his seat.

"They look like vigilantes," Felix said. "Relax, it's no big deal."

Adonis wasn't convinced. "Man, I need to cover my hair."

"Relax," Felix said. "These guys won't bother us."

"Better safe than sorry," Damiete muttered.

Osaretin reached into his seat pocket, pulled out a

hoodie, and tossed it to Adonis. "Here, put this on."

As they pulled up to the checkpoint, an officer shone his flashlight into the car. "Where are you boys headed?"

"It's my birthday," Osaretin said, flashing his best smile. "We're just going to hang out."

The officer nodded. "Who are the guys in the back?"

"My friends," Osaretin said. "And this is my sister," he gestured to Nimi.

The officer's flashlight landed on Damiete. His brows furrowed. "Guy, why your hair be like that?"

Damiete forced a smile. "Just small curls, sir."

"Step out of the car."

"For what now?" Felix blurted.

The officer shot him a look. "Are you questioning me?"

"No, sir," they all chorused.

Osaretin pulled over, turned off the engine, and got out.

"Where did you get this car?" another officer barked.

"It's my dad's," Osaretin answered.

"Who's your father?"

"Mr Garba Nurudeen, from Edo State."

"Garba Nurudeen? An Edo man with such a name?"

"We're Muslims," Osaretin explained.

The officer grunted. "Make I see your license and registration?"

Osaretin quickly retrieved the documents. He watched the officer collect it and step back to his colleagues as he scanned through the document.

At intervals they looked at Osaretin, who kept on smiling sheepishly.

Meanwhile, Damiete and Adonis whispered to each other.

"What are you two muttering about?" another officer

snapped. Nimi nudged Adonis cautiously. Immediately, he stepped away from Damiete.

"Nothing, sir," Damiete said, pressing a finger to his lips.

The officer skimmed through the papers. "Search them," he ordered.

A second officer hurried to them, patting them down one by one. When he got to Damiete, he paused, frowned, and then pulled something from his pocket, his face filled with surprise.

A folded piece of paper. He dusted it, and a fine powder trickled down.

The officer's eyes darkened. "What's this?"

He sniffed it, withdrawing it from his nose almost immediately. "Cocaine," he declared.

"Ahhh!" They all shouted at once.

"You children are pushing drugs?" The officer said, passing it to his colleague.

Damiete shivered, his hands went to the top of his head. "No, sir! That's not mine! I don't know how it got there!" He swore.

"Oh, so the officer put it in your pocket?" another officer sneered.

"No, sir! I swear, I don't know anything about that!" He was already on his knees, begging. One of the officers barked for him to stand up, but he refused, almost in tears.

Osaretin, Adonis, Felix, and Nimi stood frozen, their eyes on Damiete, completely shocked at what the officers said they had found on him.

Adonis turned when he heard Nimi sniffing, she had broken into tears, silently. If only they had just gone home.

The officer holding the paper handed it to his colleague. The second officer sniffed it and nodded.

"This is definitely cocaine. Arrest them."

Nimi's hands flew to her mouth. "Damiete?" she whispered. She could no longer hold it in, she wailed.

"Sir, please! I don't know anything about this!" Damiete kept begging as the officers pulled him off the ground, dragging him to the back of their car.

"All of you, down!" One officer barked to the friends.

They squatted.

"Sit on the floor!"

They obeyed.

Minutes later, an officer waved at the police van. "Load them up."

They pleaded, but it fell on deaf ears. Nimi's hands trembled as she quickly sent a text to her mother.

"We've been arrested. They're taking us to the station."

She was lucky enough to have clicked the send button before an officer loomed over her. "What are you doing? Hand over that phone!" He snatched the phone from her, looked at it briefly before pocketing it.

She hesitated, hoping her mother had seen the message. But whether help would come in time was another story.

At the back of the police van, their faces shadowed by the dim light, the group exchanged silent, uneasy glances.

Nimi sniffled quietly, wiping tears from her cheeks, while Adonis turned to Damiete, his face, a map of expression. He was curious, exhausted, and at the same time, disappointed.

"Please, tell us the truth," Adonis spoke out, his voice was very low. "Were you with the cocaine?"

Damiete exhaled sharply, frustration etching across his face. Convincingly, he said, "You know me. You know where I come from, my home, my family. Have you ever seen me with drugs? I don't even smoke cigarettes. I swear, I had nothing to do with that cocaine—I don't even have an idea of what it is like, talk more of carrying it. I swear, I have no idea how it got into my pocket."

A heavy silence followed, save for the rattling sound of the vehicle as it ran over potholes.

Adonis hesitated. "Do you think the officer planted it on you?"

Immediately, Felix hushed him, scared that he might be heard. "Don't make this thing get worse, Adonis. If they hear you say this, things will only get bad," he warned.

Osaretin remained silent, staring at the floor.

On the other side, Nimi sobbed quietly. "What do I tell my parents?" she whispered. "I told them I was at a friend's house. Now I texted my mum saying I'm in a police station. Oh my God."

The boys all looked at her, then turned their heads away in pity.

When they arrived, they were immediately processed—names recorded, pockets emptied, phones and money confiscated.

Then came the statements. Damiete resisted at first, but after a beating, he was forced to admit possession of a hard drug.

Minutes later, they were separated—Adonis, Osaretin and Felix in one cell, Damiete locked away alone, and Nimi placed in the women's holding area.

The stench hit Adonis and Felix before they even stepped inside. It was poorly lit and almost dark save for the little window that allowed light seep in. The air was thick with sweat, urine, and damp mold. The walls were stained with writings and ugly drawings from previous suspects who must have sought for several ways to keep themselves busy so they could stay sane. At the corner, the boys could notice water pooling.

Felix gagged. "Is this really what a police cell looks like?"

Adonis could barely breathe. "Why did they separate us?"

Felix swallowed hard. "I don't know… but we can't stay here, it is going to kill us faster than we expect."

"Ssshhh," someone in the corner hushed.

They were a little bit terrified.

Since they got in, the bodies in the cell had barely moved, except for the timely wave of the hands to ward off houseflies.

"Make una just find one corner sit down, no come here dey make noise," a voice instructed.

They scurried to a corner of the cell, straining their eyes to catch a glimpse of who must have said that, but all they could see were black-skinned bodies, sweaty and dirty.

From the dark corner which they peered into, a set of eyes stared back at them with so much viciousness that they were so quick to withdraw their gaze.

The night was agonising—mosquitoes feasted on their skin, rats scurried between their feet, and sleep was impossible.

By morning, they were exhausted, having spent the entire night trying to shoo away the rats.

Now, the situation was no better. The air remained stale, light barely seeped in, and Adonis, desperate to relieve himself, hesitated before approaching the hole in the corner that served as a toilet.

Meanwhile, Nimi lay curled on the cold, hard floor— exhausted, itching from mosquito bites, her body stiff from the dampness.

A voice jolted her awake.

"Mama, wake up. You still dey sleep?"

Blinking up at the unfamiliar woman towering over her, Nimi struggled to sit up.

"Since you be the new cellmate, you go clean this place."

Nimi stared at her, unsure if she was serious. "Clean what?"

The woman's expression darkened. "Dem no dey ask question for here."

Nimi turned her head away, willing herself to stay silent.

"You go clean abi you no go clean?"

"No," Nimi muttered.

Before she could react, the woman kicked her legs so hard that pain shot through her body. Nimi let out a small whimper.

"Say that again."

She swallowed her pride, forcing herself to stand.

"You go clean abi you no go clean?"

Nimi exhaled, still nursing the pain. "I go clean."

"Better. Oya, carry that broom, go inside toilet."

Nimi hesitated. The moment she stepped inside, the overwhelming stench hit her. Her stomach churned. So this was where the smell had been coming from.

She clenched her fists. This can't be happening.

Damiete's breath came in short, laboured gasps. The air was thick and suffocating around him. He tried to move his hands but realised they were tied behind the chair he sat on. He attempted the same with his legs, but they, too, were bound.

He cursed, straining to see through the black cloth covering his face.

Pain still racked his body from the beating he had received the night before, just before he was thrown into the cell.

He heard footsteps approaching and tried to call out—only then did he realise he was completely gagged.

His mind raced in terror. He began shaking the chair frantically, hoping to get someone's attention.

Then, two officers walked into the cell and hoisted him up. He tried to struggle, but a sharp blow landed on his face, drawing more blood.

Through the haze of pain, he heard the sound of a car door slamming shut behind him, followed by the roar of an engine.

Moments later, he felt himself being moved.

7

"Good afternoon," a yellow-skinned officer in uniform said from behind the counter. He had a faint tribal mark on his cheek and was scribbling into a notebook.

"Oga officer, good afternoon. We are looking for our children," Mr Frederick responded.

"I'm looking for my son, Adonis," Annetta added. She had walked in, scanning the faces of everyone there, hoping to spot him.

The desk officer turned to Mr Frederick. "Oga, what is your child's name?"

"Nimi Frederick," he answered without hesitation.

"Which one? Na boy abi girl?"

"A girl," Mr Frederick replied.

The officer scanned through the book, his expression shifting when he found the names. "So na your children dem catch with cocaine?" He chuckled.

"What?!" Mr Frederick's voice thundered through the station in astonishment.

"Officer, my son does not carry cocaine!" Annetta snapped, pacing sideways in frustration.

"Please, can we see them?" Mr Frederick asked, regaining

his composure.

"Oga, bail money na one hundred thousand naira. Bring your money, and you go see them."

Annetta stopped in her tracks, breaking into tears. The officer grew irritated and waved a hand dismissively. "Madam, abeg stop this cry cry," he muttered.

She ignored him, pleading instead.

Mr Frederick took a deep breath and calmly asked for the account details.

"No, oga. Na cash," the officer said flatly.

Mr Frederick and Annetta exchanged glances, surprise written all over their faces. The officer had already turned back to his book but, sensing their silence, he looked up again.

"Na so we dey do am for here. Na cash. We no dey collect transfer."

"You don't expect me to walk around with a hundred thousand naira in cash, do you?" Mr Frederick asked.

"Oga, go bank, go carry the money come."

For a moment, Mr Frederick hesitated. He knew the demand for cash was to avoid any traceable transactions—it was pure extortion. But he had no choice. With a reluctant sigh, he turned and walked out of the station, leaving Annetta behind.

About fifteen minutes later, after he had returned with the money, an officer led Adonis, Felix, Osaretin, and Nimi into the room. Their heads were bowed in shame, avoiding eye contact.

"Thank you, officer," Mr Frederick said as the officer launched into a lecture on parental responsibility.

While he spoke, Osaretin leaned towards Felix and Adonis. "Where is Damiete?" he whispered. No one answered until they left the station.

As soon as they crossed the gate, Mr Frederick's palm met

Nimi's face, sending her to the ground. She gasped, clutching her cheek as she struggled to get back on her feet.

Annetta quickly stepped in, pleading for mercy. Nimi hurried behind her for protection while Mr Frederick lashed out threats to deal with her once they got home.

"So this is the birthday party?" he spat, his eyes burning with fury. He turned sharply to Osaretin. "Do you know how many police stations we searched for you children?" He pulled out his phone, his fingers trembling with anger.

Annetta, standing off to the side, locked eyes with Adonis. He stood frozen, his face stiff with guilt. She could only shake her head in disappointment.

Mr Frederick dialled a number. "Hello, Mr Nurudeen, your son is here," he said, then hung up after a few seconds.

He turned back to the boys. "So, you're into cocaine now?"

"No, sir!" they protested in unison.

Adonis stepped forward. "We were framed. Yes, they found the cocaine in Damiete's pocket, but he didn't have any drugs on him."

"Who is Damiete?"

"Our friend. He was with us," Adonis replied.

"You mean you're not even complete?" Annetta asked, her voice laced with fresh concern

"No, ma," they answered in unison, exchanging uneasy glances.

"So where is he?" Mr Frederick asked.

"Still inside the cell," Osaretin admitted.

Mr Frederick's face darkened. "Tell me exactly what happened."

Osaretin swallowed hard. "They stopped us at Abacha Link Road junction, started asking questions, then told us to step out. After a while, they brought us here in a van."

"What time was this?"

"Around 11 PM," Osaretin turned to Adonis for confirmation.

Mr Frederick's eyes narrowed. "What were you doing there at that time? Is that the road to your house?"

Silence.

"I'm asking all of you!" Nimi's father barked

"No sir!!!" they chorused.

"So, because this is your first birthday, you decided to celebrate till 11 PM?" He turned to Osaretin, cursing under his breath.

Osaretin remained silent, his gaze fixed on the ground.

"Where did the cocaine come from?" Annetta asked.

No one spoke. Then, Nimi broke the silence. "The officer placed it in Damiete's pocket. I saw him."

Everyone turned to her in shock. The silence deepened. She glanced at their faces, knowing well that they expected her to continue.

"Before the officer searched us—while they were still interrogating us in the car—I saw one of them discreetly pass something to the officer who searched Damiete. He tried to be subtle, like he didn't want us to notice, but I saw it. At the time, I didn't realise what they were doing. Damiete doesn't do drugs. They set him up," she said firmly.

Just then, a car pulled up beside the station gates. Mr Nurudeen stepped out, Felix's father trailing behind him. Both men wore expressions of simmering rage, their faces damp with sweat.

Before he even reached his son, Osaretin, Mr Nurudeen spotted a stick on the ground, picked it up, and swung it towards him.

"You foolish boy!" he bellowed.

The stick was mid-air when Mrs Annetta and Mr Frederick intervened, blocking the blow just in time.

"Sir, please," Annetta pleaded.

Mr Nurudeen ignored her, his voice rising. "Where is my car?"

Osaretin braced himself for another strike, but his father only landed a light hit—just a warning. He knew the real punishment would come later at home.

His father's notorious temper had never stopped him from living his life, though. In many ways, he was his father's son—stubborn and unyielding.

"Are you deaf? I said, where is my car?"

"It's here in the station," Osaretin muttered.

"You'd better go and get it."

Osaretin turned, leading the way, his father following closely behind.

Meanwhile, Mr Frederick turned to Nimi. "Do you know Damiete's parents?"

"Yes," she replied. "He has a father and a sister. I know where she sells in the market."

Mr Frederick exhaled. "Since they released all of you except him, they probably want a special bail from his family. We need to inform them."

Felix's father had just arrived. He stood silently, watching. Felix wasn't surprised. His father's punishments never came in public—he saved them for home. For now, Felix was just relieved to be free.

"Nimi!" Chika, Damiete's sister, gasped when she saw her. She had been preparing to leave for the market when Nimi and Adonis arrived at her doorstep.

"Have you seen my brother?" she asked urgently.

"That's why we're here," Nimi replied.

"What happened?" Chika's voice rose in panic.

"Aunty Chika, we were arrested two days ago," Nimi said carefully.

Chika's hands flew to her mouth. "What did they say you did?"

"Nothing, Aunty. We were coming from our friend's birthday party when they arrested us. They claimed they found cocaine in Damiete's pocket."

"Jesus!!" Chika screamed, her breathing turning uneven. "So where is Damiete? You're out—where is he?"

"The police refused to release him, even after our parents paid our bail," Nimi explained.

Chika's expression darkened. "So he's still in the station?"

"Yes."

"Tell me the station."

Nimi quickly described the location.

Without hesitation, Chika packed her things, locked her door, and turned back to them.

"Where is Daddy Damiete? He needs to go with you. You can't go alone," Nimi said.

"He travelled. He'll be back in two days," Chika said, her voice laced with anxiety. "If I don't get Damiete out today before my father returns, I'm finished."

"I will go with her," Adonis said.

Nimi shot him a look. "Do you want to get arrested again?"

"Don't worry, they won't arrest me," he assured her.

With that, they set off towards the police station.

At the station, Chika's sharp eyes landed on a middle-aged

woman in a brown overall, a broom in hand. Recognising her from church, she approached.

"Mama, good morning," Chika greeted.

"Good morning, my daughter," the woman replied.

"Glory to Jesus," Chika said in the traditional Roman Catholic way.

"Honour to Mary," the woman responded.

Adonis stood back, watching the exchange.

After a few minutes of quiet conversation, Chika turned to Adonis and gave him a subtle nod. It was time to go in.

She walked straight to the light-skinned man behind the counter. He looked up, quickly noticing the grief on her face and immediately recognising Adonis, who had walked in with her.

"Officer, my brother is here," Chika said.

"Which one be 'your brother is here'?" The officer responded, feigning ignorance.

"He was arrested with his friends and is yet to be released," she said. "This is one of his friends that just left this station yesterday."

The officer took a long look at Adonis, pretending not to recognise him, then turned back to Chika. "What did they say your brother did?"

"Co… Co… cocaine," she stuttered, feeling embarrassed. Then, as though she had just realised something, she added, "But I am very sure my brother wasn't with any drugs."

"If you say your brother no carry cocaine, that one mean say e no dey here," the officer said with a smirk. "Na only criminals we dey lock up for here."

Immediately, Chika dropped to her knees, tears streaming down her face. The officer, seeing this and trying hard to avoid making a scene, quickly barked,

"Madam, go and bring a lawyer. Go and look for a

lawyer."

"Officer, please," Chika pleaded, her voice trembling. "There must be a mistake somewhere. My brother doesn't do drugs."

"Ehn, say e no do drugs no mean say e no fit carry am go give person wey dey do drugs," the officer retorted.

Chika clutched her head, mumbling through her tears. "He doesn't do drugs, he doesn't transport drugs. Officer, he no dey do anyone, na innocent pikin." She kept repeating herself in despair.

The officer scoffed. "So you mean say police dey lie? We just accuse am for nothing?"

"No, sir. Please, sir," she begged, falling to her knees.

The officer's face hardened. "Do you want to join him? Or did you not hear what I said?"

Chika swallowed hard. "Okay, okay. Can I at least see him?"

The officer didn't answer. He simply turned away, his silence a clear dismissal.

Defeated, Chika turned to Adonis. "Let's go."

As soon as they stepped outside, her composure shattered once again. She sank onto a bench, crying and shaking uncontrollably.

"What will I do?" she sobbed. "Where will I get money for a lawyer?"

She sat there, helpless, while Adonis remained silent, unsure of what to say or do.

"You don see your brother?"

Chika turned to see the woman she had greeted earlier approaching them.

"No, I never see am," she replied, fresh tears dripping down her face.

"What did they say?" the woman asked.

"They said I should bring a lawyer, that the case is serious."

The woman frowned. "Wetin dem talk say your brother do?"

"They said they found cocaine in his pocket."

The woman let out a dry chuckle. "Which cocaine?" she asked sarcastically. "Go home and come back tomorrow. I go see who I fit follow talk."

A flicker of hope returned to Chika's face. "Thank you, ma. God will bless you."

"Don't thank me yet," the woman said flatly. "I only said I'll try."

"Okay," Chika nodded, still grateful. She watched as the woman walked away.

Adonis turned to her. "I know someone who can speed up this process."

Chika wiped her face. "Let me follow you."

"No, don't worry," he insisted.

"Are you sure?"

"Yes. I'll go now and update you if anything happens."

Chika hesitated, then gave a small nod. "Okay."

She watched as Adonis disappeared into the street, clinging to the small hope that things would somehow work out.

"Good morning, sir," Adonis greeted Mr Eroboghene, who was seated on his wooden stool, eating.

Mr Ero looked up, chewing. "Ahn ahn, because of the work I give you, na why you came late?"

"It's not like that, sir. I was arrested."

"Ah, Adonis, you're now an ex-convict!" Mr Ero teased.

"What happened?"

"I was harassed by the police on my way home Friday night, arrested on Saturday, and released on Sunday."

Mr Eroboghene paused mid-bite.

One of the workers behind them called out, "That means you really be ex-convict!" The others burst into laughter, but their amusement was short-lived as Mr Ero shot them a stern look.

Leaning back in his chair, he asked, "Tell me wetin happen."

Adonis recounted the entire incident, and when he finished, Mr Ero shook his head. "These policemen—when dem go stop arresting people just to collect money? Wetin dem demand before dem go release your friend?"

"They said they needed a lawyer."

"A lawyer? For fake cocaine possession? Wetin these people dey up to?" Mr Ero muttered. Then, turning to Adonis, he said, "Bring me my phone. E dey my office."

Adonis hurried inside and returned with the phone. Mr Ero dialled a number, and a deep baritone voice answered.

"Mr Eroboghene, this one wey you remember me today, hope say all is well?" the voice said from the other end.

"My officer, good afternoon, sir. How your family?"

"They're fine. How business?"

"Business dey move well. My officer, e get one matter wey I need your help with."

The officer chuckled. "I knew it!"

"My officer, you know say your people na our eyes oh. One of my boys dey arrested on Saturday for the station, and dem no gree let am go."

"What's his name?"

Mr Ero turned to Adonis. "What's his name?"

"Damiete."

"Damiete what?"

"Damiete Apiafi," Adonis responded.

"His name is Damiete Apiafi," Mr Ero repeated into the phone.

"Okay, I'll check into it and get back to you. What was he charged with?"

"Possession of cocaine."

"Cocaine? How old is he?"

"Nineteen," Adonis quickly replied.

"He's nineteen years old," Mr Ero confirmed.

"Where did a nineteen-year-old boy see cocaine?"

"I don't know," Mr Ero admitted.

"Alright, Mr Ero. I'll look into it and get back to you."

"My brother, thank you."

"No problem," the officer said before hanging up.

Mr Ero turned to Adonis. "Don't worry. The case will be settled." He picked up his plate and continued eating.

Feeling a bit relieved, Adonis nodded and left to get back to work.

When Adonis was done and about to leave the workplace, he went on to Mr Ero. "Sir, has the officer called you?"

"I've been calling him, but he isn't answered. Maybe e busy. I'll keep trying," Mr Ero replied, then paused. "I hope your friend no really carry cocaine?"

Adonis remained silent.

Just then, Mr Ero's phone buzzed with a text. He read it and handed the phone to Adonis. "Read this."

The message read:

Oga, this your boy is in strong hands. This case is bigger than me. I couldn't find anyone by that name in the station, but I saw his record in the files this morning after you called. This is all I can tell you. Tell the family to go to the station first thing tomorrow before it's too late. Sorry, I can't pick up your call.

Adonis frowned. "Sir, I don't understand."

"Just tell this information to the boy's family. I no have anyone else I can call," he paused, collecting his phone from Aza. "Tell them to reach to the station for early morning."

That evening, Chika, who had not had a moment of rest, dialled a number. It rang, but no one picked up on the other end.

She redialled, pressing the phone to her sweaty ear.

Silently, she said a prayer while she waited for the receiver to answer.

Still, no response.

She called again, pacing back and forth. Making the sign of the cross, she murmured another short prayer, her hands trembling.

At last, the call connected.

"Hello, Mama, good evening, ma," Chika greeted hurriedly.

"Chika, nobody is talking about the boy. Are you sure he's in that station?"

"Yes, ma! That's where he and his friends were detained. The others have been released. I spoke to them this morning, and they confirmed he's still there."

"I asked my friend to check the records of those arrested over the weekend. His name is nowhere to be found. There's nobody like that in their cell," the woman said.

"My goodness!" Chika gasped, her heart pounding.

"Come to the station tomorrow and look for your brother. I don try my best, but I no find am," the woman said before hanging up.

The phone slipped from Chika's hands as she slumped onto the floor, cold sweat covering her skin.

"What will I do? What will I tell Daddy?"

She dropped to her knees, hands clasped together. "God, please save my brother. Don't let anything happen to him." Her voice trembled. "Please, God."

The moment Damiete regained a little strength, he let out a slow, muffled cry. Suddenly, the car came to a halt. He noticed the change instantly and dragged himself to a corner of the van, waiting.

His world was nothing but darkness. His hands were slick with sweat, his nose clogged with the metallic scent of blood, and his head throbbed unbearably. Pressed against the corner, he sat there, breath shallow, waiting for the sound of the door creaking open.

Outside, he heard voices—two officers deep in conversation. One was clearly a superior. Moments later, they were joined by someone who seemed to be a doctor, but their voices were faint. Straining to hear, Damiete edged closer to the window, pressing his ear against the warm steel of the van.

"Hope he doesn't have too many injuries?" the doctor asked.

"No, just a few. He struggled when we brought him here."

"Is he ready to go in?" The doctor's voice was softer.

"Yes, but one more thing..." A pause. Then, the younger officer added, "He wasn't alone when we picked him up. He had friends with him.

"How many?" The superior officer's baritone voice sent

a fresh wave of fear through Damiete's body. He flinched involuntarily, shifting his weight and making a faint noise. The voices outside stopped.

"Seems like he's awake," the doctor noted.

"Forget about his friends," the superior officer said dismissively. "It was better to take just one. If more of them disappeared, it would attract too much attention."

"Let's get him out," the doctor instructed.

Damiete heard the crunch of footsteps approaching the van. He shrank back into the corner, heart pounding, eyes darting frantically behind the blindfold covering his face. His head was spinning, but he forced himself to stay awake.

Then, the door flung open.

A rush of warm air hit his skin. Two officers climbed in, grabbed him roughly, and dragged him out. His legs trembled violently—too weak to support him. He barely felt the ground beneath him as they pulled him forward, his feet carving a long, unsteady trail in the dirt.

At last, they dumped him onto a chair. A moment later, the black fabric was yanked from his face, flooding his vision with harsh, blinding light.

A tall man, draped in a crisp white robe, stared directly into Damiete's face. His eyes held an unsettling curiosity.

Behind him stood another man—muscular, imposing— his baritone voice issuing orders with an air of authority. His face was devoid of emotion.

Damiete looked from one to the other, realising they were the same voices he had heard outside the van.

His eyes darted around, scanning the room. This wasn't the police station where he and his friends had been detained. This place was different—scanty, eerie. The walls, marked with chalk and coal, told of a building long abandoned.

"Hey! Can you hear me?" The doctor snapped his fingers

in front of Damiete's face.

He reached for the gag in Damiete's mouth, but the superior officer stopped him with a raised hand.

"No. Leave it on until you're done."

Damiete's fear deepened. His pulse hammered in his ears. Then, from the hallway behind him, a door creaked open. He turned just in time to glimpse a group of doctors wheeling someone out of a dimly lit room.

"Face forward!" the superior barked, punctuating his order with a stinging slap.

Damiete gasped, the force of the blow sending a fresh burst of pain through his head. Blood pooled in his mouth, and he spat it onto the floor. His eyes burned with tears as his body trembled violently. The throbbing in his skull grew unbearable.

Then, he saw it—the doctor, walking over from a small table, a syringe in hand.

A fresh wave of terror surged through him. He lurched forward, trying to escape, but two officers pinned him down.

"No, no, don't struggle. This will only take a second," the doctor murmured, his voice eerily calm.

Damiete, who had always feared needles, begged through the gag, but his muffled cries went unanswered.

The doctor exchanged a glance with the officers, who tightened their grip. He thrashed against them, but their hold was suffocating.

The sharp prick of the needle pierced his skin.

Moments later, the doctor pulled back, satisfied with the blood sample. He gave a slight nod, and the officers released Damiete, who slumped forward, breathless and drenched in sweat. His vision blurred, his limbs weak. Through the haze, he watched the doctor walk away, carrying the blood-filled syringe in a small metal box.

The superior officer followed close behind.

Without hesitation, the officers who had restrained him yanked him off the chair and dragged him down the hallway. Damiete exhaled deeply, as if it were his last breath, before his world faded into darkness.

A sudden splash of ice-cold water shocked him awake.

Gasping, he sat up, completely drenched. His chest rose and fell rapidly as his eyes adjusted to the dim light. A warden stood over him, holding an empty bucket. Without a word, the man turned and exited, locking the cell gate behind him.

Damiete groaned, rubbing the back of his neck. The dull ache remained, though not as intense as before. He turned his head, hoping to ease the stiffness.

His soaked shirt clung to his skin as he wrung out the water. He made to lie back down—

Then, he saw it.

The cell walls.

Until now, he hadn't paid much attention, too overwhelmed by pain and exhaustion. But now, something caught his eye.

At the top of the wall, a chilling message was scrawled in uneven handwriting:

They take us and never bring us back.

His breath hitched. He turned to the opposite wall. Another inscription stared back at him:

No one will save us.

His stomach twisted.

A low, guttural moan drifted from the darkest corner of the cell.

Damiete froze.

He had thought he was alone.

"They will kill us."

The voice wavered. A pause.

"They will kill us."

Damiete jumped to his feet, stepping back in alarm. His pulse pounded as he strained to see through the shadows.

Then, slowly, from the darkness, a boy crept forward—no older than Damiete himself.

A knock at the door startled Chika. She wiped her face quickly and pulled it open.

"Papa!" she gasped. "I thought you were coming tomorrow?"

Her father, an ageing man with deep lines of worry carved into his face, stepped inside, brushing dust off his sleeves.

"My daughter, I need to harvest my maize—it's time." His eyes scanned her face, noticing the redness in her eyes. His tone shifted. "Don't tell me Damiete isn't home."

Chika's lips quivered. She lowered her gaze.

"Papa... Damiete was arrested."

Her father froze, his grip tightening on the wooden chair beside him before sinking into it.

"Arrested? For what?"

Chika swallowed hard, her voice trembling. "They said they found cocaine on him."

His face darkened instantly. "Cocaine? My son cannot be with cocaine!"

"Papa, they're lying!" Her voice cracked as fresh tears welled up. "I went to the station yesterday, and they told me to bring a lawyer."

He shook his head, his hands curling into fists. "Where

will we get the money for a lawyer?" he muttered, his voice filled with frustration.

Chika wiped her tears roughly. "Papa, let's go and beg them tomorrow. I know it's money they want."

Her father's jaw tightened, his eyes burning with restrained anger.

He knew how the police operated in this country. He had heard too many stories—stories of boys who went in and never came out. He feared his son was about to become another one.

The next morning, Chika and her father arrived at the police station early.

The waiting area smelled of sweat and damp papers, the air thick with the quiet tension of people waiting for justice that never came.

The officer at the counter barely looked up as he flipped through a register. Then, he shook his head.

"The name is not here, Oga and Madam."

Damiete's father's chest tightened, his gut twisting. "So where is he?" His voice was barely above a whisper.

Chika stepped forward, anger flashing in her eyes. "Where is my brother?" she demanded. "I was here two days ago, and they told me to get a lawyer. Now you're saying he's not here?"

The officer shrugged. "Madam, I am telling you that your brother is not here." He turned to Damiete's father. "I will advise you to check other stations.

Chika's hands balled into fists. "No offense, Officer, but which one is it? Do you have my brother or not?"

Before the officer could respond, a senior policeman entered, flanked by younger officers. The way the others straightened and saluted him made it clear—he was the Divisional Police Officer, or someone even higher.

"What is going on here?" his voice cut through the room.

The officer at the counter gestured towards Chika and her father. "Sir, they claim someone they know was arrested and is being held in our cell."

The senior officer's gaze swept over them, sharp and uninterested. "Who?"

"My brother," Chika answered immediately.

His eyes flicked to her father, then back to her. "What is his name?"

"Damiete, sir."

A pause. Then, in a flat tone, he said, "There is no inmate in this station with that name."

He turned to leave but hesitated. "I suggest you check other stations. You are in the wrong place."

Damiete's father dropped to his knees. His voice cracked with desperation. "Oga, please, you are a father like me. Please, if you have my son, any amount you want, we will pay. Just release him."

The senior officer scoffed, barely concealing his contempt. "You want me to manufacture your son for you?" Without another word, he walked away.

The officer at the counter smirked. "Oga, all this time you've spent crying, you could have been searching elsewhere."

Chika's phone rang. She answered quickly.

"Hello, Nimi."

"Chika, what's going on? Have they agreed to release Damiete?"

"No." Her voice trembled as she struggled to hold back her tears. "They said they don't have him."

"What?!" Nimi's voice spiked with disbelief. "Damiete is there—unless they moved him. We were all together. I'm on my way with Adonis."

"No, please don't come," Chika pleaded. "I don't want anything to happen to you. I'll call you when we get home."

A tense pause. Then, "Okay, Aunty."

The call ended, and Chika turned back to the officer at the counter.

"Sir, if he was transferred to another station, please just tell us."

The officer eyed her suspiciously before muttering, "You can check Obinigba Police Station."

Before she could respond, her father suddenly bolted down the corridor leading to the offices.

"Where is this man going?!" the officer yelled, sprinting after him.

Chika moved to follow, but another officer stepped in her way, blocking her path.

Inside the Divisional Police Officer's office, Damiete's father fell to his knees, his voice raw with anguish.

"Please, sir, I'm begging you. He's my only son. Even if it's his corpse, please… just give him to me."

The DPO, caught off guard, leaned back in his chair and studied the desperate man on the floor. He said nothing for a moment, then turned to an officer.

"Bring me the list of criminals."

For the first time since hearing of his son's arrest, a flicker of hope dawned on Damiete's father.

He wiped the beads of sweat from his forehead as an officer hurried out. Moments later, the officer returned with a thick book—different from the one at the front desk.

Damiete's father watched anxiously as the DPO flipped through its pages.

"When did you say he was arrested?"

"This week."

The DPO continued scanning the list, his finger trailing down the pages. Then, an officer leaned over, pointing at something in the book.

The DPO's expression changed. He hesitated before looking up.

"What did you say his name was again?"

"Da… Damiete Apiafiii," he stammered.

A brief, tense silence filled the room. The DPO exchanged glances with the officer beside him. Then, with a straight face, he shut the book.

"Your son escaped the night he was brought here," he said flatly. "He's now wanted."

Damiete's father blinked, his mind struggling to process the words.

"Escaped?" he whispered.

The DPO leaned forward, his voice turning cold.

"If he contacts you and you don't report to us, you will be arrested."

The world tilted beneath him. His lips moved, but no sound came out. His body trembled as he sank to the floor, tears streaming down his face.

An officer stepped forward.

"Oga, stand up," he said, grabbing him by the arm. "You heard my Oga."

Damiete's father didn't move. His body felt heavy, his mind numb.

"Oga, if you no go now, you go find yourself for cell o," the officer warned.

Slowly, hesitantly, he got to his feet, wiping his face with the sleeve of his shirt. His legs felt weak as he followed the officer outside.

At the reception, Chika spotted them and rushed forward.

"Papa, what did they say?"

He raised a hand to silence her.

The officer kept walking, guiding him past the main exit.

"Let's go," he said.

Chika frowned. "Papa, what about Damiete?"

He didn't answer. He just walked.

She chased after him, her voice rising in panic. "Papa, please, talk to me!"

But he kept moving, his silence heavier than any words.

When they arrived home, Nimi, Osaretin, Adonis, and Felix were waiting outside. Their smiles faded the moment they saw Mr Apiafi's face.

"Good evening, sir," someone greeted softly, but he didn't respond.

Chika followed closely behind, stretching a trembling hand towards Nimi. The group exchanged worried glances before stepping into the living room.

Mr Apiafi sank heavily into a chair, his eyes vacant. His voice came out hollow, like a man drained of all hope.

"They said he escaped."

The room erupted in shock.

Chika's breath hitched, her pulse pounding in her ears. A storm of emotions churned within her—anger, fear, despair, confusion.

"I don't believe this…" Adonis muttered.

Everyone turned to him. He stood still, staring at the floor as if trying to make sense of it all.

Chika moved closer, shaking him slightly. "Adonis, what

do you mean?"

He inhaled sharply and lifted his head. "They beat him. Terribly."

Chika's heart clenched. She knelt beside him, gripping his forearm. "How do you know this?"

"That night… I heard someone crying. It sounded just like Damiete."

A heavy silence settled over the room.

"If he escaped, he would have contacted one of us," Osaretin said, doubt thick in his voice.

"Maybe he doesn't want to be traced," Nimi suggested. "Maybe he's hiding."

"Or maybe he's been killed," Felix murmured.

The entire room turned to glare at him.

"D-Don't say that," Mr Apiafi warned, his voice cracking. He clenched his jaw, trying to fight back fresh tears.

Nimi moved to his side, rubbing his back reassuringly.

Chika, meanwhile, struggled against the dark thoughts creeping into her mind. She refused to believe Damiete was gone. She had to believe he was alive.

But then her vision blurred. Her body swayed. A deep, cold shiver ran through her, making her limbs feel too heavy to move.

"Chika!" someone called, but the voice felt distant.

She tried to grab a chair, but her hands wouldn't obey. The room spun—then everything went dark.

She collapsed like a felled tree.

Her father lunged forward, catching her just before she hit the floor.

"Nimi, bring water!" he barked.

Nimi sprinted to the kitchen and returned with a bowl of cold water and a napkin. Mr Apiafi laid Chika gently on the ground as Nimi pressed the damp cloth to her forehead.

Osaretin, Felix, and Adonis stood frozen, the weight of the moment pressing down on them.

Minutes passed before Chika's eyelids fluttered open. She didn't move. Silent tears slipped down her cheeks.

A heavy, suffocating silence filled the room.

Mr Apiafi's voice broke as he whispered, "M…my son is gone. This is not a country of justice. My son is gone!"

"We can't just leave it like this. We have to do something!" Adonis said firmly.

Mr Apiafi turned to him sharply, his grief twisting into frustration.

"And what can you do?" he snapped. "You're just kids!" His voice wavered between anger and helplessness. "Please… go home."

He stood and gestured towards the door, his face lined with the weight of a father's worst nightmare.

That night was long and filled with sorrow.

Deep down, they all knew justice was a distant dream. But how would they find Damiete?

That night was long and filled with sorrow. Deep down, they all knew justice was a distant dream. But how would they find Damiete?

Chika lay awake, tossing and turning. This isn't real. This can't be real. Just days ago, her brother had been here, buried in his books, studying for his JAMB exams. Now he was gone. How?

Unable to sleep, she slipped out of bed and crept to the living room. Her father was still there, sitting motionless on the couch, staring into the distance. The television buzzed in the background, but he wasn't watching. He wasn't really there.

Early in the morning, Chika was up and dressed.

She stepped into the living room and found her father in the same position.

"Where are you going?" he asked as soon as he saw her.

Chika straightened. "Good morning, Papa. I'm going to the station. They have to tell me where my brother is."

"My daughter, please sit down."

"Papa, I know you're old, and you think there's nothing we can do—"

"Shut up!" he snapped, his voice sharp with frustration as he got up. "You think I'm stupid? That I don't know the right thing to do?"

Chika clenched her fists. "I am not like you. I can't sit back and watch my innocent brother vanish into thin air!"

Her father let out a bitter chuckle. "And what exactly do you plan to do when you get there? Attack the policemen? They'll kill you, Chika. And **NO ONE WILL DO ANYTHING ABOUT IT.**"

She froze, seeing that her father had given up completely. She was disappointed, and for the first time, she grew hate for her father as she watched him take his seat. He looked exhausted, she could tell.

"So are we going to do nothing about this?" She asked.

"Let us wait and pray, he will contact us one way or the other." her father said. He bowed his head into his palms and sighed, praying that his faith doesn't let him down.

Chika sank into a chair, burying her face in her lap. She hated that he wasn't doing anything. She hated that her father would rather wait, with faith suspended over his head like the tongues of fire, than go in search of her brother.

Meanwhile, at Adonis' house, the television crackled to life with Pere sitting in front of it.

"Eighteen positive cases from fifty tested patients have been recorded in Lagos within the last 24 hours," a news anchor reported.

Pere turned up the volume, listening intently to the reporter.

"In response, the CDC and the government have announced a mandatory 14-day lockdown in hopes of containing the spread. If the situation worsens, authorities may be forced to extend the restrictions indefinitely."

Adonis, who had been seated in the room watching the news, exhaled. He rubbed his temples, finding it difficult to concentrate while his mind raced to the missing Damiete.

"A lockdown, now?" he muttered. The world was falling apart, and amidst it all, Damiete was gone.

Mr Pere let out a loud hiss. "I'm sure this COVID-19 thing isn't even in the country. But trust the government to turn every situation into a cash grab. How did the virus get here? Weren't all borders shut and flights canceled last month? Please spare me," he scoffed, looking at Adonis, who stared at the news reporter blandly.

Adonis nodded slightly. It made sense. The country had pulled too many stunts over the years for anything to be surprising anymore.

"Those people in the isolation center might even be getting paid to say they have the virus. But what do we know?" Mr Pere added.

That statement made Adonis chuckle, but it was short-lived. The weight of everything that had happened kept the laughter trapped in his throat.

Just then, Annetta burst into the sitting room, panting.

"What is it?" her husband asked, startled.

"The police chased us out of the market! They're taking this lockdown seriously. They were even harassing people without masks," she said, breathless.

"Woman, didn't I tell you this morning not to go out?" Mr Pere snapped.

"I bought one on my way home. I didn't think they were serious! I just wanted to get some vegetables for yam sauce," she defended.

"You would've been making it in jail if they had arrested you," Pere said sarcastically. But no one laughed. Nothing was funny.

Noticing Adonis' unusual silence, she turned to him. "What's wrong?" she asked.

Adonis couldn't hold it in any longer. "Damiete is missing."

The room fell silent. A stillness so deep, it felt like time had stopped.

"What?" Annetta whispered.

"His father was told at the station that he escaped the night he came in." He looked up at his confused parents, shock melting over their faces. "I don't believe he escaped from that cell. I think they made him do something very terrible."

Annetta gasped, placing both hands over her mouth. She walked up to Adonis and patted him in a comforting way.

"This is sick," she murmured. "I'm sure that boy will be alright."

"Adonis, you need to be careful now. I don't even know who we're supposed to be hiding from anymore—police, ritualists, kidnappers, thieves…" Pere said.

But Adonis barely registered the warning. All he felt was rage. He wanted justice for Damiete.

But how?

Liverpool, England

It was the last day of school. Nioma and her friends had planned a house party at Amanda's place to celebrate.

Excitement bubbled inside her—she was finally done with high school and ready for college. But deep down, she knew what that meant: her mother would probably send her far away, claiming it was to help her focus on school.

But Nioma knew better. Her mother just wanted her out of the way—so she could focus on her politics and little boys. Every night, she woke up to strange noises from her mother's room, and by morning, she'd watch her mother see off another man—usually one in ripped, low-cut jeans, the kind a twenty-five-year-old would wear.

Watching her mother go through them like disposable toys was both frightening and depressing.

There were times she wanted to call her sister, to tell her everything. But if her mother found out, there would be hell to pay. So, Nioma did what she always did—kept her mouth shut and pretended she saw nothing. She just needed to get out of that house.

As she grabbed her bag and headed for the door, her mother called out, "Make sure you're back by 10 PM."

"Okay, Mum," she replied without looking back.

Her mother had ordered a ride for her, but Nioma wasn't thinking about the party. Not really.

Her mind was on Ivan.

They had been talking for a while now, and every time they were together, her body reacted in ways she barely understood. The rush of emotions, the heat under her skin—it was all too much. She had spent so long being scared, holding herself back.

Tonight, she wanted to be free.

She wanted to feel like a woman.

And she wanted Ivan's hands on places that had never been touched before.

Nioma arrived at Amanda's house. The moment she stepped inside, she spotted Amanda, Jessie, Lola, and a few classmates doing a strange, almost choreographed dance.

The music was blasting, and the air was a concoction of perfume, sweat, alcohol, and marijuana.

She took a quick glance around the dimly lit room, searching for Ivan. Instead, she spotted his friends huddled in a corner, laughing loudly, drinks in hand. But no Ivan.

"I guess you're looking for Ivan?"

She turned to see Lola standing behind her, smirking.

"Hi, Lola. Nice party," Nioma said, forcing a smile.

Lola pulled her into a hug. "We're finally done with high school!!!!!"

"Yeah, yeah," Nioma giggled before lowering her voice. "Did Amanda's parents really organize this?" she asked, looking around, taking in the entire party with her eyes.

Lola scoffed. "Of course not. They're out of town for the weekend."

"Ah… I see," she nods.

"Come, I want to show you something."

Before Nioma could protest, Lola grabbed her by the wrist and led her to where a group of girls were lounging. A thick cloud of scented smoke hung over them. The girls took turns in smoking from a pipe.

"Have you ever smoked shisha before?" Lola asked.

"No. Why would I?"

"Come on, it's harmless."

Nioma hesitated. "I don't think so."

Lola gave her a knowing look. "Oh, stop acting brand-new. We know about the pills."

"What?!" Nioma's heart nearly stopped.

Before she could react, a familiar voice interrupted them.

"Hi, ladies. Hi, Lola. Hi, Nioma."

Nioma turned, and for a moment, it felt like a bolt of lightning had struck her head.

Ivan.

Thank goodness he's here, she thought, suddenly aware of how fast her heart was beating.

"I thought you weren't coming," she said, trying to sound casual.

"I was here before. Just stepped out to see someone," Ivan replied smoothly. Then, taking her hands in his, he added, "Can we talk?"

As he led her away, he threw Lola a wink. "I promise to bring her back."

Lola arched a brow, watching them suspiciously. "She is all yours," she called out.

From across the room, Amanda's voice rang out, "I hope everyone's having a good time?"

The crowd cheered in response.

Nioma barely registered the comment. Amanda winked at her just as she and Ivan slipped out through the front door.

They sat on a wooden bench outside, the distant sound of music humming through the walls. The cool night air wrapped around them, but all Nioma felt was the warmth of Ivan's hands—one resting on her lap, the other slipping around her waist.

"So, I guess it's finally legal for me to date you now?" Ivan teased, his voice low and playful.

Nioma burst into laughter. "I don't know about that."

"Come on, you know I've been waiting." He leaned in slightly. "Do you have any idea how long I've wanted to hold you like this? To never let you go?"

Nioma smirked. "Are you planning to kidnap me?"

"Of course not… unless you want me to."

They both laughed, their voices blending into the night.

Just then, a motorcycle rumbled past the house. The rider's helmet visor was up, revealing a face that looked eerily familiar.

Nate, her usual supplier.

For a split second, their eyes met, and a flicker of recognition passed between them. But before she could process it, he was gone.

She faced Ivan, adoring every ounce of him while he spoke.

Lost in thought, she barely noticed as his face inched closer. His pointed nose grazed her chin before his lips pressed softly against her neck. A shiver ran down her spine. His grip tightened, pulling her closer to him.

She pulled back slightly, locking eyes with him. Then she smiled, and he did too.

Of all Ivan's features, his smile was her weakness.

He may have been a white boy, but nothing about him screamed white—not his charm, not his mannerisms. He had a confidence, a smoothness, something that felt effortlessly cool.

And right now, in his fitted sweatshirt, he had never looked more attractive as it hugged his muscular frame just enough to make her pulse race.

Tonight, he was all hers, she thought to herself.

"Do you want to go to the garage?" Nioma whispered into Ivan's ear.

"Right now?" he asked, eyebrows raised.

"Yes, unless you have somewhere else to be."

"Of course not."

Without hesitation, Ivan took her hand and led her towards the garage. They slipped inside, pulling the door shut behind them. A worn-out sofa sat against the wall, and they wasted no time sinking into it.

Just as Nioma opened her mouth to speak, Ivan silenced her with a kiss.

"No more talking," he murmured against her lips.

She nodded, heart pounding.

His lips moved hungrily against hers, his hands exploring her body with slow, deliberate movements. But while he was lost in the moment, she hesitated—her hands remained folded in her lap, too nervous to touch him.

Ivan's lips trailed from her mouth to her cheeks, then down her neck, leaving a burning sensation in their wake.

Then, out of the corner of her eye, she saw something.

A face.

For a split second, she was sure it looked like Nate—the pills guy.

Her breath hitched, and she bolted upright, her pulse now racing for an entirely different reason.

"What's wrong?" Ivan asked, his body stiffening.

"I thought I saw someone at the window."

Ivan turned to glance at the small garage window, but there was nothing there.

"It's probably just one of the guests," he said, trying to reassure her. "Maybe we should go inside, somewhere more private. What do you think?"

Nioma swallowed hard. The mood had shifted, and she couldn't shake the uneasy feeling creeping over her.

"I'm sorry, Ivan, but I'm not in the mood anymore."

"Oh… are you sure?"

"Yes, I'm sure. Let's just go back to the party. I don't feel good—I'm sorry for dragging you out here."

Ivan studied her for a moment before nodding. "It's nothing. Let's go back."

They left the garage, the moment between them slipping away like smoke.

Nioma's phone buzzed for the tenth time that night. Her mum.

She sighed and picked up. "Mum, I know. The ride is outside. I'm coming."

Hanging up, she turned to her friends. "I have to go."

Amanda, Lola, and the other girls hugged her, showering her with goodbyes. Ivan, standing a little apart from the group, stepped closer and pressed a kiss to her forehead.

"See you later?" he asked.

She smiled. "Yeah. Later."

The car headlights flashed as she slid into the backseat, shutting the door behind her.

As soon as the car pulled away, she dialled Nate's number.

"Hello, hello," he answered on the first ring, his voice smug.

"Are you stalking me?"

"Of course not," Nate said smoothly. "Just following my money."

Her stomach twisted. "How much do I owe you? I'll get it ready."

"I think you already know. Or… I could come by your house to pick it up."

"No! Please don't. My mum would kill me."

Nate chuckled darkly. "Then meet me at the usual spot with my money, slut."

"I'm not a slut."

"Whatever, slut."

The line went dead.

Nioma's fingers tightened around her phone as her pulse hammered in her ears.

It was late. Too late.

If she wasted any more time, her mum would start asking questions.

"Please drop me here," she said to the driver.

The man glanced at her through the rearview mirror. "We're not at the destination yet. It's just one more block."

She exhaled sharply and stayed silent until they reached her house.

"We're here, ma'am," the driver announced.

"Yeah, I know," she muttered.

Just as she stepped out, her phone buzzed again. A text from Nate.

NATE: You just pulled up at your house. Want me to come over?

She hissed, texting back.

NIOMA: No, I said I'd meet you at our usual spot.

"Your payment has been made, ma'am. Have a good night," the driver added before pulling away.

Her phone rang again.

"Hello, Mum. I'll be up in a minute—I'm in the backyard."

"Oh, okay," her mum replied, her voice laced with mild suspicion.

Nioma hung up, taking a deep breath. Tonight wasn't over yet.

She took a good look at her building and the dark street. Without hesitation, she turned around and sprinted to the spot where she would meet Nate.

"Where are you?" she asked, panting heavily.

"Right behind you," he replied.

She spun around, scanning the darkness. "I don't see you."

"Beside the church."

She turned towards the old Eighth Century Church and spotted his bike parked in the shadows. As she ran up, she found him crouched behind it.

"Why are you playing hide and seek?" she snapped, stretching out her hand. A few coins sat in her palm. "This is all I have. I have to go."

"Slow down, now. I've got new stuff—this one's dope," he said cunningly, waving a sachet of some strange drug.

"I don't have money for that."

"Relax. First one's free, on me."

He popped a pill into his mouth and offered her another. Without thinking, she took it and swallowed it almost immediately.

"Damn, tiger, slow down," Nate chuckled. "You know, when I saw you with that dude earlier, I was kinda jealous."

Nioma tensed. "So you were stalking me?"

"Just wanted to watch some soft porn."

Her eyes flew open. "What the hell are you talking about?"

Nate stepped closer, his smirk sending a chill down her spine.

"Back off!" she snapped.

"You sure, honey? You were ready to get some tonight." He drew close to her.

"Please, just leave me alone. I have to go home—my mum will be looking for me." She shrugged, pushing him away.

"Bullshit." His voice turned cold. "You know your mum doesn't care about you. She's probably in bed with one of her sons.'"

A sharp pang shot through Nioma's chest. Before she could react, a strange heaviness settled over her limbs. Her vision blurred. Her heartbeat slowed. She felt herself becoming paralysed in seconds.

"What… is this?" Her voice was weak. "What did you give me? Why do I feel—"

Her knees buckled.

She felt herself falling, sinking into darkness.

Nate caught her before she hit the ground, lowering her onto the cold pavement. A twisted grin crept onto his face.

"I promise this'll be your best night."

He unfastened his belt, pinned her down, and yanked her pants off.

Then he forced himself into her.

But something was wrong.

"The fuck?" He bit his lip, pressing harder. "This bitch is a virgin?"

She stirred weakly beneath him, her body barely responsive.

Still, he didn't stop.

Each thrust stole more of her breath, her presence fading until she was completely still.

When he finally finished, he leaned down, brushing his lips against her ear.

"How does that feel?"

Silence.

"Nioma?"

Still silent.

"Nioma, wake up." He kicked her softly.

Still no response.

"Come on, don't play with me." He shook her roughly. "I know my dick is good, but wake the fuck up."

He pressed his fingers to her neck.

No pulse.

His stomach dropped.

"Oh, my fucking God." He stumbled backwards, his breath ragged.

"What the hell? This drug wasn't supposed to…" He wiped the sweat forming on his forehead. His hands were shaking.

"What do I do? What should I do?" He paced frantically, his mind racing.

Then, headlights.

A car was coming.

Panic seized him as he bent down, dragging Nioma's body towards a garden behind the church. He shook her one last time.

Still, she didn't wake.

Without another thought, he grabbed his motorbike and pushed it away from her lifeless body.

As the car neared, he broke into a sprint, disappearing behind the Eighth Century Church.

Leaving her behind in the dark.

"Nioma!"

Ann jolted awake, her daughter's name tearing from her lips. Her heart pounded as she threw off the covers and slipped into her robe. She hurried to Nioma's room, pushing the door open, hoping to see her daughter tucked in bed.

It was empty.

The bed looked untouched, as if no one had slept in it.

"Where is this girl?" she muttered, frustration rising.

She rushed to the kitchen and checked the back door. It was locked. A chill ran through her.

If the back door was locked, and the front door was too, that meant…

She never came home last night.

Ann's hands shook as she checked her phone. No missed calls. No messages.

Panic set in. She flung the back door open and ran to the garage. No sign of Nioma. Heart racing, she dialled her daughter's number.

No answer.

She tried again. Still nothing.

On the third attempt, someone picked up.

"Nioma! Where the hell are you?"

A deep voice responded. "Ma'am, this isn't Nioma. This is the police."

Her breath caught. "What? Where is my daughter?"

"Ma'am, could you come to the Eighth Century Church, near Overbury Street?"

"What happened?" she demanded.

But the line went dead.

Ann sped to the church, still in her nightdress, her pulse hammering in her ears. As she arrived, she stumbled upon the scene of what looked like an accident.

The blaring sirens. The flashing police lights. The small crowd forming.

A sinking feeling gripped her chest.

She whispered a prayer as she pushed through, rushing towards the officers.

"Please! Wh… wh… where's my daughter?"

Then she saw it.

A stretcher. A body, covered with a white sheet.

Her legs nearly gave way. She moved forward, but an officer blocked her path.

"Ma'am, are you the mother of Nioma?"

Ann's gaze darted between him and the stretcher. The world blurred. She could barely register the officer's words.

She opened her mouth to speak, but all that came out was a cry.

The officer stepped aside.

Slowly, she walked towards the covered body. Her hands trembled as she reached for the sheet.

With bated breath, she pulled it back.

Her breath hitched.

"Nioma!! No! No! No! Please, wake up! Your mum is here! Don't leave me! Don't leave your sister!"

Her cries echoed through the morning.

A female officer knelt beside her, gently holding her as she sobbed.

"Ma'am," the officer whispered, "I'm so sorry, but we need to take her body for forensics."

Ann clutched her daughter's lifeless hand, her world shattering around her.

IMPUNITY

8

donis, Felix, and Osaretin sat in the empty classroom after lessons, chatting idly when Nimi walked up to them.

"Guys, are you not ready to leave? I'm heading home," she said, adjusting her backpack.

Osaretin stood up immediately. "I'm ready, let's go."

"I think I'll hang around for a while," Adonis said.

"Me too," Felix added.

"Alright then, see you guys tomorrow." Nimi waved and walked off with Osaretin.

A heavy silence settled between Adonis and Felix.

"Things just aren't the same without Damiete, you know?" Adonis muttered. "It's been a while now, and no one has heard anything about him. I still find it hard to believe he escaped the cell that night." His fists clenched on the desk. "I want to do something, but I don't even know what. I'm just angry."

"I believe there might be something they are hiding from us," Felix said quietly.

"So he'll just go like that? No one held accountable?" Adonis shook his head. "That's crazy."

At that moment, Reana entered the classroom. She looked uneasy, scanning the room before walking up to them.

Two boys followed her in but hesitated at the door, exchanging glances before turning and walking out.

"Are you okay?" Adonis asked.

Reana hesitated, then sat beside them. "I don't know why they want to talk to me," she said.

"You don't know them?" Adonis asked.

She shook her head.

"Those guys are bad news," Felix said. "You need to be careful.

"I was leaving when they approached me," Reana explained. "I ignored them, but they followed me. Who are they?"

"They're cult boys," Adonis said flatly.

Her forehead creased. "What do they want from me?"

"Maybe one of them likes you," Adonis shrugged.

"But I don't like them," she snapped.

Felix and Adonis exchanged a look and burst into laughter.

"Just be careful," Adonis repeated.

Reana exhaled, glancing towards the door. "Can you guys walk me to the gate? I need to get a cab."

Adonis and Felix nodded. They walked with her to the school gate, waiting as taxis passed by, none willing to pick up a single passenger.

"This isn't working," Felix muttered.

"Let's take a mini-bus," Adonis suggested. "We're all going in the same direction anyway."

Reana hesitated, then shrugged. "Alright."

"I know this seems unusual for you," Adonis said after they boarded a bus.

"What?" Reana asked.

"Making use of public transport."

"Not really," she said. "Whenever I run out of pocket money, I take a bus or taxi."

"Oh… okay. But still, not like me. This is my everyday ride," he chuckled.

"It's cheap."

"Yeah, and uncomfortable," Adonis grumbled. "Not to mention, we're inhaling bacteria straight from the conductor's mouth—and this is COVID-19 period."

Just then, the bus bumped into a pothole. He turned to her and smiled; she laughed.

Reana chuckled. "I still can't believe there was an actual lockdown. Two weeks indoors? I was bored to death."

"It was crazy," Adonis agreed. "I haven't even met anyone who had COVID-19, though."

She turned to him. "You expect to see them walking around on the streets?"

He smirked. "I mean, no one I know has had it. It kind of feels… fake."

She scoffed. "I pray you get it so it feels real to you."

His eyes widened. "Wait—was that a curse?"

Reana laughed. "Not at all. You just don't believe it's real, so maybe experiencing it will help."

Adonis shook his head. "I know you don't like me, but you don't have to make it so obvious."

"You're just picking words out of my mouth," she teased.

He leaned back. "You ignored me a few weeks ago when I tried talking to you. But now you need a bodyguard, and suddenly, I'm useful?"

"Please don't hype yourself," she rolled her eyes. "Meeting you in that classroom was just a coincidence. I was looking for an escape route."

"You really don't like me, do you?"

"No, I'm just being honest."

Adonis sighed, then smiled playfully. "At least tell me your name since I'm now your bodyguard."

She smiled. "Fine, if it'll stop your whining."

"Oh, wow. Really?"

She chuckled. "Relax. It was a joke. My name is Reana."

"Rihanna? Like the singer?"

She rolled her eyes. "No. R-e-a-n-a."

"That's a cool name. I'm Adonis."

"I know."

"Oh? But you acted like you weren't listening before."

"I just have a good memory," she said with a smirk. "Anyway, tell the driver I'm stopping at Heritage Bank ahead."

"Got it." Adonis turned to the driver. "Heritage Bank, please."

When the bus stopped, Reana pulled out some money and handed it to the driver.

Turning back to Adonis, she smirked. "I paid for you— consider it your first salary as my new employee."

Adonis laughed. "Really? Okay, boss."

Reana stepped off the bus, tossing a final glance over her shoulder. "See you tomorrow, Adonis. Thanks."

He grinned. "See you."

As soon as Reana stepped off the bus, her phone rang. She glanced at the screen—her mother.

"Mum? What's wrong? Why are you crying?"

"Where are you?" Ann's voice trembled. "What I'm about to tell you… please keep it to yourself. Don't tell Aunty Julianna or your father."

Reana's heart pounded. "Okay, Mum. What is it?"

There was a pause, then her mother's voice cracked.

"Nioma is dead."

Reana froze. "What? Who?"

"Your sister," Ann whispered. "She was murdered last night."

Reana slapped a hand over her mouth as a scream tore through her throat. Passersby turned to stare, but she didn't care. The world around her blurred.

No. This wasn't real.

She gripped her phone tighter, her breath coming in gasps. She knelt on the floor, sobbing. After a while, she picked up the phone and asked in a teary voice, "Why? Who would kill Nioma? What did she do?"

"I don't know… She was coming back from a house party, and then…" Ann's voice trailed off; she had already started sobbing.

"Then what, Mum?" Reana's voice rose. "How did you let this happen?"

"What are you talking about?" Ann's grief turned sharp with anger.

"Mum!" Reana shouted, stepping off the curb without looking.

A car horn blared, jolting her back to reality as a driver swerved past her. She barely noticed.

When Reana got home, the aroma of dinner filled the house. In the kitchen, Aunty Julianna stood at the stove, stirring a pot.

"Sweetheart, you're back," she said with a warm smile.

"Yes, Aunty."

"How was the tutorial today?"

"Okay," she answered blandly.

Julianna paused, watching her. "Are you alright?" She

noticed the tear tracks on her face.

Reana nodded and headed straight to her room, slamming the door behind her.

She fell onto the bed and began sobbing, muffling the sound with her pillow to keep her aunt from hearing and walking in.

Then there was a knock on her door. She swiftly turned her head and realised she had forgotten to lock it. Heart racing, she ran to the door and turned the key, shutting the rest of the house away.

The next day, as Reana arrived at the tutorial centre, she was surprised to see Adonis standing at the gate.

"What are you doing here?" she asked.

"I'm waiting for my boss."

"Who?"

Adonis smirked. "Remember? You hired me yesterday."

Despite herself, she managed to smile. "How are you?"

"I'm good. But you don't look too well. What's wrong?"

"I'm fine," she lied.

"You sure?"

She raised a brow. "Are you trying to be my therapist now?"

They walked into the compound together. As they passed the security post, Reana noticed the same boys from yesterday—the ones who had followed her—sitting there, chatting idly. They stopped talking the moment they saw her and Adonis, their stares lingering.

Reana frowned. "Why are they looking at me like that? I wonder what they want."

Adonis shrugged. "You're hot and cute. What don't they want?"

She rolled her eyes. "Was that a compliment?"

"Perhaps."

"Do you always like beating around the bush with girls?" she asked.

"Maybe I'm just a bush man," he said jokingly.

She shook her head, a small chuckle escaping despite the heaviness in her chest.

They sat on a bench in the classroom, waiting for the teacher to begin, when Felix walked in hurriedly. He stopped at the entrance of the class and scanned it, then spotted Adonis and Reana at the far end. He waved at them and walked over.

"Hey, is there a space for me?" he asked.

Reana nudged Adonis.

"No," Adonis said, smirking. Then he turned to her. "Wait, you don't want him to sit here?"

"No."

"Why?"

"I don't like him."

Adonis frowned. "Felix is cool."

Reana hesitated, glancing at Felix as he found another seat. "I don't know… there's just something about him that feels off."

"Reana, wake up. The class is over."

She blinked, disoriented. "I didn't even realize."

"Of course, you didn't." Adonis sighed.

"I'm tired, Adonis," she murmured. "I'm just… so tired."

Adonis, who had already stood up, hesitated, then sat back down. His voice softened. "What's wrong? At least tell me something."

Reana exhaled shakily. "I just lost my younger sister."

She paused, then, almost in tears, whispered, "She was killed."

Adonis froze, his lips parting in shock. Immediately, he took her palm and pulled her close, wrapping her in a hug as she broke down in tears.

"It's okay," he murmured.

Reana lifted her head, her eyes burning with anger. "My mum is the reason this happened!"

Adonis pulled back slightly. "Why would you say that?"

She looked away, refusing to answer.

"Do you want to stay for the next lecture, or should we go somewhere private?"

Reana wiped her eyes and stood, grabbing her bag. "Let's go."

They strolled behind the church building, near the hall used for the tutorial sessions. One of the church members organised the classes, so the space was always accessible. Beneath a mango tree, they sat on a wooden bench in silence.

Adonis pondered what to say. He felt the need to talk to her—maybe it would help ease the pain—but he feared making her more upset. She was in a delicate state. So, he stayed silent, just watching her cry.

About thirty minutes later, Adonis' phone rang. Felix.

"Bro, hwfa?" Adonis answered.

"Where are you?" Felix asked.

"Reana and I went for a walk."

"Oh wow," Felix chuckled. "Didn't know you two were dating now."

Adonis quickly lowered the phone's volume, glancing at Reana. She had already stopped crying and gave him a weak smile.

"It's nothing like that," Adonis said, rolling his eyes.

"No worries, man. I guess I'll see you tomorrow—

hopefully without Reana." Felix laughed before hanging up.

Reana stood up. "I think I want to go home now."

"Why? Are you upset about what Felix said?"

"No, I'm just tired. I need to rest."

Adonis studied her for a moment, then sighed. "I know this is weird for me to say since we just met, but if you ever need someone to talk to, don't hesitate to reach out to me."

Then, gently, he leaned forward and hugged her, tightening his grip around her. She tightened her grip in return and smiled.

"Let's go," he said.

When Reana arrived home, she heard muffled sobs from the living room. Her chest tightened as she rushed inside.

Aunty Julianna was on the floor, weeping.

Reana's stomach dropped. Mum must have called.

"Aunty?" She hurried to her. "What is it?"

Julianna looked up, her face streaked with tears. "My sweet baby… come here." She opened her arms, pulling Reana into a tight embrace.

Reana whispered, "I know."

Julianna pulled back slightly, her eyes wide. "You know what?"

Reana's throat tightened. "I know Nioma is dead."

Julianna gasped. "My God, Reana! Why didn't you say anything?"

"Mum said she would call you herself." Reana swallowed hard. "Did she tell you what happened?"

Julianna hesitated, then nodded. "Yes, she did. Reana… it's bad."

"Please," Reana pleaded. "I deserve to know."

Julianna took a deep breath, her voice barely above a whisper. "Your sister was drugged and raped. She overdosed on whatever they gave her."

The room spun.

Reana shot up from the couch and ran straight to her room, sobs wracking her body.

"Reana!" Julianna followed, but before she could reach her, Reana slammed the door shut, locking herself inside.

For days, she barely spoke—to her aunt, to her mum, to anyone.

Julianna tried to reach her, but Reana shunned her every time.

And just like that, the world around her faded into silence.

A month after the JAMB exams, Reana received the news she had been waiting for—she had been admitted to the University of Port Harcourt to study law. The moment she saw it, excitement surged through her, and she sprinted to the living room, where her cousins and Aunty Julianna were sitting.

"I'm going to Uniport to study law!" she shouted.

At first, they were startled—surprised that she could feel joy again.

"How did you find out?" Joan, her eldest cousin, asked.

"My friend helped me check the results!"

"I'm so happy for you! You've always wanted to study law," Julianna said, beaming. But deep down, she was even happier about something else—Reana had smiled again.

"This is great news," she added. "You should call your

mum and dad."

Immediately, Reana's mood changed. She lowered herself onto the couch beside Peter, Joan's younger brother. "Maybe later," she muttered.

Julianna opened her mouth to say something, but Peter shot her a look, silently telling her to let it go.

"Now you can finally put bad people in jail," Julianna said, forcing a smile in an effort to lighten the mood.

"Yes," Reana smirked. "I can finally put corrupt politicians behind bars."

A brief silence followed.

Peter stole a glance at his sister and mother, both staring at Reana with wide eyes. She definitely meant her father—Aza Kio Briggs.

Later that evening, after watching a movie with her cousins, Reana disappeared into her room. When she returned, she was dressed and ready to go out. She stepped into her aunt's room.

"Aunty, I'm going out with my friends. We want to celebrate our results."

Julianna smiled. "Okay, sweetheart. Just be home on time."

"I will."

"By the way, that's a nice dress," Julianna added.

Reana smiled. "Thank you, Aunty."

She was wearing a navy and aqua blue dress that complemented her dark skin, letting her hip-length braids flow freely down her back. She paired the outfit with silver heels and a pearl-studded dark purse—one of her favourite gifts, given to her on her 18th birthday.

"I know that's right!" Joan hyped her up.

Peter grinned. "Where are we going?"

Reana raised a brow. "We? Nowhere. I am going out with my friends."

Peter sighed dramatically.

"At least let me take a picture!" Joan pleaded, already holding up her phone.

After countless pictures—and Joan's satisfied squeal—Reana was finally free to leave. She and Adonis had agreed to meet at the West End Hotel.

When Reana arrived at the hotel, she spotted Adonis at the bar, dressed in jeans and a crisp white T-shirt.

He had a strong, broad exterior, and though he was only 5'7", there was something about him that made him stand out—like he wasn't as young as the rest of the guys from the tutorial centre.

"Hi, Adonis," she called.

Adonis turned around—and froze. His eyes widened, and for a moment, he just stared.

Reana chuckled. "Come on now, we've been dating for a while. Don't act like you didn't already know I'm pretty."

Adonis finally snapped out of it, shaking his head with a grin. "You're pretty, that's for sure. But is that why I had to wait an hour for you?"

Reana gasped. "Nooo! It hasn't been an hour... or has it?" She looked at her watch.

Adonis rolled his eyes.

She laughed. "Okay, maybe just a little bit. But trust me, it was worth the wait."

A few hours later, they lay on the bed, watching a movie in one of the hotel rooms.

"Are you sure you can spend the night here?" Adonis asked, his voice laced with concern.

"Of course," Reana assured him. "My aunt is working tonight, and I already told my cousins I wasn't coming back."

"Okay," he sighed. "I just don't want you to get into any trouble."

Reana turned to him with a soft smile. "Don't worry, I'm fine. Let's just enjoy our first night together."

Adonis chuckled. He studied her face for a moment, then smirked.

"I still don't get why we have the same nose, though."

"Adonis, stop," she groaned. "You say that all the time, but mine is more pointed."

"You always want to claim the finer things," he teased. "But seriously, we kinda look alike."

"We don't. I'm pretty. You're not."

"I'm not because I'm handsome."

"Maybe forty percent."

"Yeah, yeah," he sighed dramatically. "At least you're with the forty-percent handsome dude. I can manage."

Reana threw a pillow at him, and before long, their playful banter escalated into an all-out pillow fight.

When they finally collapsed back onto the bed, breathless and laughing, Adonis turned to her. Without a word, he kissed her. He started to pull away, but she held him in place, unwilling to let go.

Adonis pressed his lips against hers again, slow and deep, sending a shiver down her spine.

She had been kissed before, but this was different. This time, she understood what she felt—and it felt good.

She parted her lips, tentatively tracing the edge of his mouth with her tongue. Adonis smirked before cupping her face in his hands, kissing her with a passion that sent warmth pooling through her. But as the moment deepened, something unsettling stirred in his mind—a lingering thought he couldn't shake.

He ignored it. Instead, he let his hands explore, gliding over the smoothness of her thighs. The slight hitch in her breath made his pulse quicken.

He moved between her legs, his fingertips brushing against her underwear.

She gasped.

Adonis froze.

"What?" she whispered.

"I thought... you didn't like it."

"No," she breathed. "I do."

He hesitated, then kissed her again, slowly, deliberately. His hands found their way back, but as his lips trailed downwards, that same uneasy feeling crept in. It was distracting, gnawing at him, and no matter how hard he tried, he couldn't push it away.

Reana sensed the shift. "Are you okay?"

"I am," Adonis murmured. "I just... I want to be sure you're okay with this. I know it's your first time."

Reana hesitated. "I don't know." *Could it be that she felt the same way?*

Suddenly, an image of her sister flashed in her mind. The pain. The injustice. She never had the chance to experience love. The gift of her first time was stolen from her.

Reana swallowed the lump in her throat and backed away. She turned onto her side, curling into Adonis's chest. Without hesitation, he wrapped his arms around her, holding her as if afraid she'd slip away.

For a long while, they stayed like that, wrapped in silence. Then, softly, Reana asked, "So what happens next for you? You're still not sure about university?"

Adonis sighed. "Reana, I have no one to support me. I don't want to be a burden to my family."

"Why would you say that? You can at least try going to a polytechnic. You can't just waste your life in that workshop."

"I'm not wasting my life," he defended. "And even if I did go to university, I couldn't study Physics. It has to be Architecture. Maybe I'll write JAMB again, but for now, I'm taking a vocational training course."

"Adonis, I know your passion is architecture," Reana said gently. "But you could accept Physics and switch to Architecture later."

"Hmmm," he hesitated. "I'll think about it," he said. "Right now, I just want to enjoy this moment with you."

Reana smiled. "I might not know what the future holds, but I do know one thing—I want to be with you. Promise me you won't leave me when I start university."

"Of course not," he said without hesitation. "I'm not like other guys. You know I'm not easily swayed."

"I know," Adonis said, but his expression was serious. "Still, I don't have much. I can't take care of you the way I should. And you might meet some rich dude in school and forget about me."

Reana rolled her eyes. "Adonis, I grew up in wealth. There's nothing new."

"You promise?"

"Cross my heart."

Adonis exhaled, finally allowing himself to relax. "I love you, Reana."

She smiled. "I love you too."

And with that, they drifted off to sleep in each other's arms.

Around 2 AM, Adonis jolted awake at the sound of voices outside.

Reana stirred beside him. "Did you hear that?"

"Yeah," he murmured, sitting up. "Someone's talking downstairs."

Reana listened closely. "It sounds like more than one person."

Adonis got out of bed, walked over to the window, and peered outside. Below, the hotel security guard stood with a few attendants, engaged in a hushed conversation.

"Is everything alright?" Adonis called out from the third floor.

One of the attendants looked up. "Nothing, Oga," he replied quickly.

Adonis wasn't convinced. Something about the man's tone seemed off. Without a second thought, he grabbed his jacket. "I'll be back. Just stay here," he told Reana.

She frowned. "Where are you going?"

"I just want to check what's happening downstairs."

"Why not let security handle it?"

"Don't worry," he said, already heading for the door.

Reana exhaled sharply. She admired Adonis's boldness, but sometimes, he was too fearless for his own good.

Not one to be left behind, she quickly dressed and followed him downstairs.

By the time she reached the reception, Adonis was already questioning the security guard.

"What happened?" he asked.

The guard glanced at the hotel attendants before

replying, "Oga, you didn't need to come down. Everything's been sorted."

"What exactly was sorted?" Adonis pressed.

Seeing he wasn't going to drop the matter, the guard sighed and lowered his voice. "There was a break-in, but I managed to stop one of the thieves with my dog. The other got away."

Adonis's brows lifted. "Are you serious?"

The guard nodded. "Yes. I called the police, and they just left about ten minutes ago."

Adonis looked down at the guard's dog, now sitting obediently at his feet. "Your dog must be really smart."

"He is. When I heard movement near the fence, I stayed hidden and waited. As soon as they jumped in and moved towards the reception, I let the dog loose."

"Wait—didn't they have guns?"

"They did, but they never fired. I don't think they had real bullets."

Adonis let out a low whistle. "You must be well-trained."

The guard chuckled. "Not exactly. I'm an ex-con."

Adonis blinked. "Seriously?"

"Yeah, but before you ask—I was wrongfully detained."

Adonis's mind immediately went to Damiete's death. He'd always wanted to understand what truly happened behind bars. This could be his chance.

"Mind sharing your story?" he asked.

The guard eyed him for a moment, then shrugged. "Why not?"

Adonis turned, ready to step aside for the conversation, but then he noticed Reana standing by the reception door, arms crossed. He shook his head. "I should've known you wouldn't stay put."

Reana smirked. "Did you really think I'd wait in the room?"

Adonis sighed. "Listen, I need you to go back inside. I promise I'll tell you everything later."

"Why? What are you trying to find out?"

"Just trust me on this, okay?" He lowered his voice. "Please."

Reana rolled her eyes. "Fine. But make sure you come back soon."

"Yes, ma'am," he said, bowing his head in mock obedience.

She playfully smacked his arm before turning back towards the stairs.

Once she was gone, Adonis focused on the guard. "Alright, let's talk."

The security guard sat comfortably on his front porch, soft music playing in the background. Adonis settled beside him, watching the dimly lit surroundings.

"This job must be stressful for you," Adonis said.

The guard let out a dry chuckle. "Yeah, not really. I could have gone for something safer if I'd been given the chance, but it was the only job I could find after my release."

Adonis turned to him with keen interest. The guard noticed, then said, "I was used in replacing a convicted murderer."

"What?!" Adonis sat up straight, his eyes wide with shock.

"Yes. Not everyone in prison is actually a criminal. I was just in the wrong place at the wrong time."

Adonis took a deep breath. "What was your experience in prison like?"

The guard leaned back, exhaling slowly. "When the judge sentenced me to ten years, it felt like a bad joke. "The night I was arrested, the guys who saw me being taken in assured me I'd be out in no time. They thought the police just wanted a bribe. We were raided at a bar, and before I knew it, I was at a correctional facility, cuffed and in uniform."

He paused, shaking his head. "At first glance, the place looked like a mini paradise—neat compound, flowers everywhere. But inside, it was a different world." He laughed bitterly. "I kept asking myself—what the hell am I doing here?"

Adonis listened intently. "What was it like?"

"A whole lot of messy things," he said, laughing as he reminisced. "Do you know that from the moment I stepped in, I got threats from some inmates? Initially, I didn't see it as something to worry about." He adjusted himself on the seat. "You know, it's normal to feel threatened in prison because everyone wants to show superiority. But it's different when you start getting threats of rape."

He paused and chuckled. "I had never been in such a situation before. At first, these prisoners were nice to me, unlike the others, but when I was being taken to their cell and asked for sex, I realized they were nice because they needed something in return."

"So did you do it?" Adonis asked.

"Do what?"

"The sex. Did you have sex with any of them?"

The guard looked up at Adonis, disappointed he had asked. He got up and unbuckled his belt, loosening its grip around his waist.

"These things are just too small," he was complaining about the belt wound around his waist.

"Did you do it?" Adonis asked again, cutting him off.

"Of course not! Why would you think I did such a thing?"

Adonis raised a brow. "Well, you said you were threatened."

"I had to scare them away. I told them I had syphilis, and they let me be."

Adonis laughed at his trick to ward off threats.

The guard smirked. "There was also a hierarchy there. Inmates with money could get anything—better food, phones, drugs. Even girls were brought in to satisfy their urges."

Adonis sat up, stunned. He had only stayed a night in a cell and had no idea things like this had happened. He stared at the guard with curiosity.

Adonis exhaled, shaking his head. "This is insane."

"You don't know the half of it," the guard continued. "I also heard about inmates being drugged and raped. Never in my life did I think I'd have to watch over my shoulder because of that. From that day on, I was scared to eat because the wardens helped carry out these atrocities."

He rubbed his upper arm, remembering the difficult nights he had endured. "But you know, one has to get used to an environment like that. I had to lie all the time to keep those vultures off my back."

Adonis shuddered at the thought.

"The most horrific of them all was the death room."

Adonis's ears perked up. "Death room?"

The guard nodded. "Everyone feared it. Once you were thrown in there, you were left to die. If the beating you received before being locked up didn't kill you, something else would—either the stench, the heat, the starvation, or the mosquitoes. But one thing was for sure—you never came out alive."

He leaned towards Adonis and spoke in a hushed tone. "If you somehow survived all that, they assumed you were a dying inmate and finished the job themselves."

Adonis let that sink in. Then he asked, "What happens to the dying inmates?"

The guard smirked. "I heard they kill them and harvest their organs. People pay a lot for that, you know." He smiled, then added, "The rich ones."

Adonis covered his mouth in shock. Immediately, his mind rushed to Damiete. He shook his head, as if trying to rid himself of the horrifying image of Damiete sliced open. He turned back to the guard, his expression pleading for more answers.

"No one ever reported the death room to the public after getting out?"

"No one. All we have to bank on is an assumption of what the death room looked and felt like. But no one ever went in and made it out alive." He paused, rubbing his dog. "The wardens threatened us with it. They told us gory stories about what our fate would be if we were thrown in there. So, we had nothing as evidence even if we wanted to speak— none of us who heard those stories had actually been there and survived."

He reached for a bag and pulled out a chunk of meat, tossing it to the dog.

"I also heard the death room was in another location, one no one knows about."

"No one ever asked about these people? Not even their families?" Adonis asked.

The guard laughed. "That's easy for the wardens. They just tell the families the inmate escaped from prison. And that's how the case is dismissed."

Adonis was taken aback. He felt his chest tighten, his hands trembling as he clenched them into fists to steady himself. He couldn't believe his ears. Panic shot through him.

Knowing he had heard enough, he stood up and walked

away in silence, leaving the guard surprised.

Back in the hotel room, the thought of Damiete still lingered. The story of the death room echoed in his head.

Reana, already lying on the bed, sat up as he walked in.

"Hey! How did the conversation go?" she asked.

Adonis sighed. "Since Damiete's disappearance, I've been curious about what really happened to him. I find it hard to believe he escaped the cell." He paused, gathering his thoughts. "A part of me still wants to know exactly how he died. So when the security guard mentioned he was an ex-con, I got curious." He exhaled. "What I heard tonight wasn't pleasant."

Reana studied his face. "What was it?"

"I think Damiete didn't escape. He might have been killed."

Her eyes widened. "What? Don't say that."

Adonis sat beside her on the bed and ran a hand over his face. "Let's forget about this for now. Tonight is supposed to be about us—good memories, not bad ones."

Reana wasn't convinced. "I know that. But I'm not a child, Adonis. There's a reason I'm going to study law. So, tell me."

"No, Reana." He looked at her seriously. "You can't fight this system. It's too` corrupt. If you try, they'll either throw you in jail or kill you. Please."

Reana laughed. "Seriously, I'm not afraid of them."

"I know." His expression softened. "Can we go to bed now?"

They lay down, wrapped in each other's arms, slowly kissing until they finally fell asleep.

9

While Reana was in school, Adonis kept himself busy with various architectural projects under his boss, Mr Ero.

One morning, as he was getting ready for work, his phone rang.

"Where you?" Mr Ero's voice came through the line.

"I'm on my way," Adonis replied, flashing his mother a playful grin as she sat at the dining table.

"I go reach office in five minutes. Hurry up—I get a new job for you, and it needs sharp-sharp attention."

New jobs always excited Adonis, and this was no exception. He quickly finished his meal, said his goodbyes, and hurried out of the house.

When he arrived at the workshop, Mr Ero was in his car, reading some documents.

"Good morning, sir."

"Adonis, you're here," Mr Ero said, glancing up. "I have a house remodelling project for you."

Adonis felt a slight twinge of disappointment—it wasn't a fresh project.

Ever since he started working full-time, all he'd gotten were remodelling jobs. Still, he was in no position to complain. He always reminded himself: *A little more time, and I'll have my own workshop.*

"Okay, sir. Can I see a picture of the building?"

"We dey go there now," Mr Ero replied. "But I get appointment at 10 AM, so come in."

Adonis quickly got into the car.

They drove through the Government Reserved Area, past its more developed sections, and into a more isolated part of it. Eventually, they arrived at an old warehouse, flanked by two uncompleted buildings about three meters apart.

Mr Ero pulled up in front of it.

Adonis studied the structure—only two windows and a central door. The place looked abandoned. What could anyone possibly want with this building in the middle of nowhere? he wondered.

"This is it," Mr Ero said, nodding towards the warehouse.

"What are we remodeling it into?"

"I never sure yet," Mr Ero admitted.

Adonis raised a brow. For a contractor, Mr Ero was unusually vague about the details.

"The senator wants to convert it into a modern warehouse with an office," he explained. "I told him I had the perfect person for the job. He said he'd explain in detail when he meets you. Look around—do you think you can work with this?"

Adonis disliked remodeling jobs, but he needed the money—for his family, for Reana. He wasn't in a position to be picky.

"Yes, I can make something out of this."

"Good. He go meet us here tomorrow. The building go dey open by then."

They walked around for a few minutes before heading back.

The next day, when Adonis and Mr Ero arrived at the warehouse, the senator was already there, seated in front of the building with two other middle-aged men. A young boy was clearing the overgrown bushes nearby.

"Senator, you're early," Mr Ero greeted, approaching the man with a chin full of white beard and streaks of grey on both sides of his head.

"I wanted to clear the area before work begins. You know I need this done quickly," the senator replied, flashing a smile that revealed bright white teeth.

"Good morning, sir," Adonis greeted, giving a respectful nod.

"This is the architect wey go handle the remodel," Mr Ero said.

The senator eyed him. "He looks rather young to be an architect. You're not bringing me an apprentice, are you?"

Adonis clenched his jaw and lowered his head slightly, hiding his irritation.

Mr Ero let out a hearty laugh. "Work with him, and you'll see that I brought you the best. You sabi my work, and I fit tell you say this young man nah e be brains behind most of my new projects."

The senator studied Adonis for a moment before nodding. "Alright, let's see what your boy can do. But I reserve the right to withdraw my proposal if I'm not satisfied."

"Absolutely," Mr Ero agreed.

The senator turned to Adonis, who was already scanning the site. "This is an old warehouse, and I need it remodeled into an office and storage space—with a basement."

Adonis turned to Mr Ero, then back to the senator, who stood confidently with his arms crossed.

"Adding a basement might require demolishing parts of the structure," Adonis noted.

"I don't mind tearing the whole thing down if necessary, but I'm pressed for time."

"The basement will have to be at the center of the building, away from the perimeter walls. That's going to take time."

"I understand—that's why I'll be bringing in extra hands."

Adonis nodded. "Alright, I'll come up with a sketch by tomorrow and send it across."

"It would be better if you carry it come in person," Mr Ero interjected before turning to the senator for confirmation.

"Yes, I'd prefer that," the senator agreed.

Something about the senator's demeanour unsettled Adonis, but he pushed the feeling aside. He had a job to do.

Without another word, he got to work, taking measurements of the existing structure. When he was done, he approached Mr Ero, who was speaking with the senator.

"You fit go back to the workshop—I go meet you later," Mr Ero said.

"Okay," Adonis replied.

With one last glance at the senator, he turned and walked away.

On his way to the workshop, Adonis stopped by a supply store to pick up some Arch D paper for his drawings. As soon as he arrived, he headed straight to the studio, where his usual drawing table was.

He started with the basement floor plan, designing a two-room compartment with doors leading to a sitting area, a staircase connecting to the upper floors, and an opening into the main building's corridor. There was also a restroom and an office, with all doors opening into the sitting area.

Next, he laid out window wells, drainpipes for the sewer system, and the basement raft foundation.

He also included an exit tunnel leading to ground level outside the building—an escape route in case someone ever got trapped down there. Oddly enough, he decided to keep that detail from the senator, though he couldn't quite explain why.

For the main building, Adonis designed a three-storey: two full levels in the middle and a rooftop chamber with a chimney. Each storey had two large storage areas, an office, a restroom, and a stairwell leading to the next level. The rooftop chamber was open and wall-less, ideal for conference meetings. He added more windows, an entrance porch, and a main staircase.

By the time he finished, he realised that the only major structural changes required would be adding extra windows to the sides and back of the building and demolishing the two existing compartments inside.

Just as he was going over the final details, he checked his watch—Mr Ero was yet to come in. It was already 7 PM.

He waited another hour for Mr Ero to review his progress, but when he didn't show up, Adonis packed up his drawings and headed home.

The next morning, Adonis received a call from Mr Ero instructing him to meet at the warehouse, where the senator was already waiting. Without delay, he got ready and took a taxi to the Government Reserved Area.

After 45 minutes in traffic, he arrived at the site and was immediately puzzled. Several cars were parked in front of the building—far more than he expected.

Was there a party inside?

Scanning the vehicles, he searched for Mr Ero's car but didn't see it. He did, however, recognise the senator's brown Mercedes-Benz. That confirmed it—the senator was inside.

Adonis approached the warehouse cautiously. Strangely, there was no noise coming from within.

He stepped inside quietly, and as he moved deeper into the building, he heard hushed voices coming from one of the compartments. He edged closer, trying to make out their conversation, but the words were too faint.

Suddenly, the voices stopped. Footsteps approached the door near where he was standing. Heart pounding, Adonis quickly pressed himself against the wall.

The door opened slightly. After a moment, the person inside seemed satisfied that no one was there and retreated.

Adonis wasted no time. He slipped off his shoes to avoid making noise and hurried out of the building. Circling around to the side, he noticed a small window he hadn't seen during his initial survey. Carefully, he leaned in. This time, he could hear them clearly.

The men inside were speaking in a coded language—deliberately vague, yet undeniably secretive.

Then, one voice said, "The fridge will be in the basement. That's the only place it can be."

Another added, "The real supplies will be stored on the top floor where the offices will be. As soon as the organ comes in, it gets registered as supplies and then moved to the fridge in the basement."

Adonis nearly lost his footing. "Organ? What did that have to do with a warehouse?" he muttered.

A chill ran down his spine. From the moment he met the senator, something had felt off—but this? This was beyond anything he could have imagined.

A phone rang inside the building. Someone answered.

"I'm on my way," the caller said.

"Don't bother, we're almost done," a man inside replied.

Then another call came in. This time, Adonis recognised the senator's voice.

"Okay, I'm at the building waiting for you, but your boy isn't here yet."

That had to be Mr Ero.

Adonis heard movement. Footsteps. They were coming outside.

Thinking fast, he moved along the wall, jumping into one of the unfinished buildings next to the warehouse. From there, he had a clear view of who was leaving.

The senator stepped out first, followed by a man in a plain polo and jeans. They stood talking, their backs turned to Adonis' hiding spot.

One by one, the men got into their cars and drove off—except for one. He stayed behind, still in conversation with the senator.

When he finally turned around, Adonis' stomach dropped.

It was the light-skinned officer with a tribal mark who always sat at the counter of the police station they were once locked up in.

"Damiete..." Adonis whispered involuntarily, recalling the name of his missing friend.

The pieces started falling into place.

He remembered the story the hotel security guard had told him—that DPOs, police officers, and cell wardens were involved in human organ trafficking.

Adonis' blood ran cold. Whatever was happening inside that warehouse, it wasn't just illegal.

It was monstrous. And he was dangerously close to the heart of it.

Adonis wasn't sure what to make of what he had just witnessed, but one thing was certain—he needed more information about the senator's plans for the warehouse.

He cautiously stepped out of the unfinished building where he had been hiding, making sure the other men had vacated the premises.

As he walked towards the warehouse, something on the wall caught his eye. A sign, positioned near the spot where he had been eavesdropping earlier, read:

SEIZED BY THE EFCC. KEEP OFF.

Adonis frowned.

Why would someone be renovating a property seized by the government?

Everything about this situation felt off.

Deciding not to confront the senator alone, Adonis walked to the front of the building and waited for Mr Ero. He had no intention of getting caught in a conversation with the senator that could jeopardise the deal before his boss arrived.

Five minutes later, Mr Ero pulled up in a taxi.

"Adonis, what you still doing outside? The senator are waiting for you," he said as he stepped out of the car.

"Yes, I know. I wanted to wait until you arrived so we could go in together," Adonis replied.

Mr Ero gave him a puzzled look. "Na wa for you. I thought you for don finish by now."

As they started towards the entrance, Adonis hesitated. "Sir, this building has been sealed by the EFCC," he blurted out.

Mr Ero paused. "How you know that?"

"It's written on the wall at the side of the building. I think it was also on the front, but someone must have painted over it."

Mr Ero scoffed. "This man is a senator. You think he no know what he's doing? Besides, you forget the country you dey? That kind thing na just for the news—it's all politics."

Adonis fell silent. He understood exactly what Mr Ero meant. In this country, anything was possible.

Inside, the senator welcomed them with a warm yet calculating smile.

Adonis spread his drawings on a table in the centre of the room—the same place the senator and his associates had held their earlier meeting.

He explained the design concept, carefully detailing each section of the building.

The senator clapped his hands in approval. "I love this!"

Mr Ero beamed. "I tell you I has the best."

The senator reached for a file on the table and handed it to Adonis. "I want you to take a look at the initial government proposal for the warehouse project."

Adonis took the file eagerly, flipping through its pages.

"I really love your design," the senator continued, "but we need to align it with the government's requirements first." His smile felt forced. Adonis shot him a wary glance.

"I want the third floor to have an open space where the agricultural incentives will be stored," the senator added.

As he spoke, Adonis skimmed through the file. The first few pages contained standard project details. But when he reached the middle, something caught his attention. The project had originally been awarded in February 2015—some years ago.

At first, that didn't seem too unusual. But then, he noticed something odd. The project had been assigned to a different recipient. On the sixth page, it was stated that the funds had already been disbursed—years ago. Yet, on the first page, a more recent date was listed, with a higher amount allocated this year.

He flipped back to the first page and read the title:

Continuation of Distribution of Agricultural Incentives to Local Farmers in Rivers State.

His grip on the file tightened.

The senator returned after surveying the space with Mr Ero. "I thought you were walking with us," he said, his tone slightly irritated. "I was just explaining what I wanted to your boss."

Adonis quickly composed himself. "Sorry, sir. I was just checking how to integrate your requests into my design."

The senator gave him a sharp look, but Adonis handed the file back without hesitation. "I'll make the necessary adjustments in the final model."

"Good. I want it ready by tomorrow," the senator said.

"Yes, yes, it'll be done," Mr Ero replied before Adonis could answer, as if he were the one doing the work.

Adonis simply stood there, processing everything he had heard and seen.

The senator suddenly turned to Mr Ero. "I need a word with you."

Mr Ero nodded. "Adonis, wait me outside."

Without hesitation, Adonis stepped out.

Once he was gone, the senator turned to Mr Ero, lowering his voice. "This boy—are you sure he's alright?"

Mr Ero let out a loud laugh. "Yes, senator. Why you ask?"

"Can't you see the way he acts? I like his work, but I don't know what to make of his character."

"He's fine. Just a young man wey wan become something. Plenty matter dey e head, that's all. Trust me."

The senator narrowed his eyes. "I don't want any surprises."

"There won't be, senator," Mr Ero assured him.

The senator nodded. "I'll send you half the payment this evening."

"Thank you, senator," Mr Ero said, trying to hide his excitement. He rarely accepted half payments upfront, but this was different. This time, he was willing to be patient. After all, the patient dog eats the fattest bone.

When Adonis got home, he couldn't keep his thoughts together. His mind wandered far. He thought about the possibility of Damiete being one of their victims. Even though he pinched himself, begging his mind to stop spiralling into negative thoughts, the very appearance of the police officer made it difficult to believe that Damiete was safe—just waiting for the right time to make contact.

Frustrated and filled with self-guilt, he picked up his phone and, without overthinking it, tweeted to his over ten thousand followers:

Imagine designing a warehouse, only to realise you're actually drafting plans for a morgue—one hiding the government's darkest secrets.

It only took a couple of minutes before his comment section started buzzing. Then the reposts surged, and the views skyrocketed. It was happening faster than he had expected.

At first, fear gripped him when he saw the sheer engagement the tweet had sparked. But then, like a sudden gust of wind, the fear was swept away, replaced by a strange sense of bravery.

Even though he had used a pseudonym, he felt like a whistleblower who had done the right thing.

Soon, an influencer quoted his tweet, adding:

Aren't we all just pencils in the hands of the government?

Adonis couldn't help but smile at the attention. He opened the tweet again and read it several times, a slow grin spreading across his face.

Later that day, when he logged back in to check the tweet's progress, a direct message popped up from an unknown account:

Delete the tweet.

Adonis ignored it. But minutes later, another message arrived—this time, a threat.

Take it down now, or face arrest.

He smirked. Lol. *You want to arrest me over a tweet? Who are you? Show yourself if you're so bold.*

The reply was immediate.

You have five minutes.

Instead of backing down, Adonis doubled down. He tweeted:

I'm being threatened by this account—@blackfolu. Apparently, tweeting about how a senator is disguising a morgue as an agricultural project is a crime now.

The tweet gained even more traction. But before users could engage with the mysterious account, it vanished— deactivated.

An hour later, loud knocks echoed through Adonis' house.

"Adonis, open."

It was Mr Ero.

Adonis opened the door, surprised to see his boss standing there so late. "Sir? What are you doing here?"

"I just got off the phone with the senator. He needs the work. Now."

Adonis' stomach twisted. *Hope this isn't about my tweet.*

"But why the urgency?" he asked, frowning.

"Stop asking questions and bring it out," Mr Ero snapped, his usual easygoing demeanour gone.

"I'm not done with the AutoCAD version," Adonis hesitated.

"Just give me the paperwork."

Adonis walked to his room, unease gnawing at him. Who was behind that account?

His mother's voice interrupted his thoughts.

"Who is that?" she asked sleepily from her bedroom window.

"It's just my boss, Mum. Go back to sleep," Adonis reassured her.

She hesitated. "At this time of night? I hope everything is fine."

"Yes, Mum. Just handing over some work."

With a tired sigh, she returned to bed.

Outside, Adonis handed the sheets to Mr Ero.

"Is this the everything?" his boss asked, flipping through the pages.

"Yes," Adonis replied, suppressing a chuckle at Mr Ero's grammatical slip.

"I go send you something for morning," Mr Ero said before speeding off.

"Something?" Adonis scoffed. His boss had covered his AutoCAD training, but that didn't mean he shouldn't be paid in full. Still, his mind was elsewhere—on the senator, the Twitter account, and, most importantly, his friend's death.

In the middle of the night, a flicker of light outside his window jolted Adonis awake.

Probably just a neighbour, he thought—until he heard a loud crash.

Before he could react, men stormed into his room. His first instinct was robbery. But then he saw the uniforms—Police.

His mother was on the floor, pleading, her cries ignored as the officers grabbed Adonis and dragged him outside.

Neighbours stirred from their sleep, watching helplessly as the van sped away.

Collapsing onto the cold floor, his mother sobbed. "What has Adonis done again?"

Street chairman Mr Donald arrived moments later. After hearing what had happened, he promised, "I'll go to the station first thing in the morning."

Adonis' fate, however, was already being decided elsewhere.

This time, Adonis wasn't afraid. He knew exactly why he had been arrested, but what shocked him was how easily police officers could barge into someone's home and take them away without cause.

In developed countries, the police came with an arrest warrant, explained the charges—but here, the law bent to the will of those in power.

Alone in a dark, damp cell, he waited. Two hours passed in silence. Just as he started to doze off, a flashlight pierced through the darkness, blinding him.

"It seems you're eager to die," a voice sneered.

Adonis squinted, but the officer's face was hidden behind the harsh glare. The voice, though—it sounded familiar.

The officer tossed Adonis' phone at him.

"Delete the tweet. Then, you're going to tell us how you got that information."

Adonis unlocked his phone, hesitated for a moment, then deleted both tweets.

"Start talking," the officer ordered.

Adonis said nothing.

A sharp slap cracked through the silence, sending a sting across his cheek.

"Talk, or you'll die in this cell," the officer threatened.

Before he could process his next move, the officer's phone rang. With a curse, the man turned and hurried out, leaving Adonis with a throbbing knot on his forehead. He bent his head, pressing a hand to the bruised skin.

Morning came, signalled by the faint glow of blue light filtering through a small opening in the cell. Distant voices chanted, growing louder by the second. Adonis strained to listen but couldn't make out the words. He tried peeking through the hole, but all he got was a wave of a deadly stench. Irritated, he spat.

Outside, Mr Donald, the street chairman, had mobilised a protest. Residents gathered at the police station, their chants demanding Adonis' release. The commotion attracted even more people—some had no idea who Adonis was or why he had been arrested, but they joined in anyway.

The police are the enemy. That was reason enough to protest.

Inside the station, the darkness of the cell remained unshaken, as if daylight never reached it. The door creaked open, and an officer entered, his face concealed behind a black mask.

Grabbing Adonis by the collar, the officer growled, "This is your last warning. Count today as your lucky day."

Adonis met his gaze, eyes burning with unshed tears.

"If you ever post about the senator again—on social media, anywhere—or speak a word about him to anyone, be prepared to take your last breath," the officer warned. "Along with your boss. And your family. We're watching you."

With that, he yanked Adonis to his feet and shoved him out of the cell.

The moment Adonis stepped outside, the crowd erupted. In jubilation, they blocked the station entrance, obstructing a red Venza that was pulling out from a nearby parking lot.

Half-smiling, Adonis watched as the driver in the tinted Venza honked aggressively, seizing the first chance to speed off, scattering the crowd in his path.

His mother rushed to him, sobbing. "This boy, do you want to kill me? You are all I have! Please don't let them take you away again."

"Mum, I'm so sorry. It was just a misunderstanding."

"A misunderstanding again?" she snapped. "Wasn't it a misunderstanding that led to your friend's disappearance?"

Mr Donald and a few men gathered around him.

"What happened there?" they asked.

But Adonis couldn't tell them the truth. Not even his

mother. His mind raced with new fears—not just for himself, but for his parents. For his boss.

Why would the senator threaten Mr Ero if he was still working for him? Did Mr Ero know more than he let on?

One thing was clear—Adonis had to tread carefully.

Later that afternoon, Adonis made his way to the workshop.

Mr Ero was welding an iron gate when he saw him. His eyes widened at the sight of Adonis' bruised face.

"What do you—?" he started, then paused.

Adonis studied his boss' face. If Mr Ero knew anything, he was hiding it well.

"You should be the one telling me," Adonis replied.

Mr Ero shook his head in frustration. "Yesterday, the senator call me, dey curse me, put threat for your head. I try ask wetin go wrong, but he just dey blame me. Say he no wan make you follow am do work again. I even beg am say make I give am another person, but e no gree."

Adonis frowned. So, he really doesn't know?

"I was arrested in the middle of the night," Adonis admitted. "They tortured me and let me go this morning—only because my neighbors protested."

Mr Ero's eyes widened. "I pass station this morning. I see the crowd. Na you?"

"Yes."

Mr Ero's reaction seemed genuine. He really had no idea.

That was all Adonis needed to know.

IMPUNITY

10

Julianna and Reana were in the kitchen making dinner when Reana's phone started ringing.

"Reana, your mum's calling," Julianna said.

"Okay."

The phone rang a couple more times before going silent. Julianna turned to Reana, her brows furrowed.

"Why aren't you picking up?"

"Nothing, Aunty. Don't worry, I'll call her back later."

"I'm worried," Julianna said softly. "Ever since your sister passed, your relationship with your mum has changed so much."

"If she wanted a relationship with me, she would have come home and explained why she neglected my sister," Reana snapped.

"Don't say that! Your mum would never neglect her child."

"You clearly don't know her," Reana said bitterly.

Julianna sighed. "I know her, Reana. She's my sister. And I know that when the time is right, she will come home."

"Yeah, whatever," Reana muttered before storming out of the kitchen.

She sat on her bed, trying to calm down when her phone buzzed. Adonis was calling.

"Hello, baby," she answered.

"I'm outside," Adonis said.

"I'm almost ready. I was about to eat."

"Babe, I'm taking you out. Why do you need to eat?"

"I thought we were going to a hotel?"

"Don't they sell food at hotels anymore?"

"Fine," she chuckled. "I'll be out in a minute."

Julianna entered the room and found Reana getting dressed.

"Going out again?"

"Yes, I am."

"You've been seeing this boy a lot lately. When are we meeting him?"

Reana smiled but didn't respond immediately. "When the time is right," she finally said, hugging her aunt before heading out.

She wore a black bandage dress that hugged her curves and nude sandal heels that made her legs look longer. As she stepped outside, every eye in the compound turned to her—including Adonis, who was waiting in a taxi.

Reana slid into the car, and Adonis couldn't take his eyes off her.

"Who are you trying to kill?" he teased.

"You," she smirked.

"Well, I'm ready to die peacefully in your arms."

They both burst into laughter. The taxi driver, caught up in their energy, tried to join in, but one look from the couple shut him down. The awkward silence was brief, as Adonis and Reana quickly got lost in murmured conversation.

At the hotel restaurant, they dug into steaming bowls of goat meat pepper soup and yam.

"You know," Reana smirked, "you've been to jail more times than a thief. Maybe you should hire me as your lawyer in case you get arrested again."

Adonis chuckled but then grew serious. "Honestly, being detained twice wasn't fun. It made me realize how many innocent people might be locked up in those cells."

Reana wiped her mouth with a napkin. "Remember that night we stayed at the hotel? I spent time talking to the security guy."

"Yeah, I remember."

"I always wanted to visit a prison just to see what it's like, but after your second arrest, I'm not so sure anymore. I never want to be in that kind of environment." She paused. "Guess what?"

"What?"

"I got offered a job at an AutoCAD and Revit Training Institute."

Reana's eyes widened. "What? Since when? Why didn't you tell me?"

"I got the mail last week."

"Wow! So you get to do that while still making furniture on the side."

"Yeah. But honestly, it's been tough getting customers since I parted ways with Mr Ero. I've had a few jobs here and there, but not enough to get my own place."

Reana placed her hand over his. "Babe, look at how far you've come. It's a gradual process. You even got this job without a university degree. You can do so much more—with time, the business will pick up, and then we can get an apartment."

Adonis raised an eyebrow. "We?"

Reana grinned. "I meant you can get an apartment… where I can visit anytime I want."

"Of course," Adonis chuckled, squeezing her hand. He hesitated for a moment, then asked, "When I ask you to marry me, will you say yes?"

Reana's eyes twinkled. "Are you proposing right now?"

"Not yet, but I want to be sure that when I do, your answer will be yes."

She smirked. "When you actually ask, I'll give you an answer I know you'd want to hear."

"Fair enough," he smiled. "So, do you want to hang around here for a while or head somewhere else?"

"I'd rather chill. We could book a room," Reana said. "I don't feel like walking around in these heels."

Adonis glanced down at her feet. "Oh, right. Those killer heels. How could I forget?"

As soon as they entered the hotel room, Adonis pressed Reana against the wall, his body moulding into hers as he captured her lips, kissing her zealously.

"I know you've been waiting for this," she whispered against his mouth.

"Yes, I have. I can't pretend any longer."

He lifted her hands above her head as if they were in his way, their kisses growing hungrier. The wall trembled as their bodies collided with intensity. Adonis spun her around, pressing her to the wall while his hands roamed freely—one cupping her breast, the other fumbling with the clasp of her bra. It slid off effortlessly, leaving her bare. He kissed the nape of her neck, sending shivers down her spine. Within moments, her dress pooled at her feet.

Adonis turned her to face him, their bodies flush against each other. Reana let out a soft moan, disrupting the last shred of restraint he had left. He dropped to his knees, sliding her panties down, then scooped her up and carried her to the bed.

They had two steamy sessions before Reana noticed daylight peeking through the curtains. Adonis lay beside her, sleeping soundly. She reached for her phone and froze— twenty missed calls. Her aunt. Her cousins. And one from her father, who hadn't called in over five years.

Her heart pounded. *What does he want?*

Just as she was about to wake Adonis, her phone buzzed again. She picked up immediately.

"Where have you been? I've been calling all night! You had me worried sick!" Julianna's voice pierced through the speaker.

"I'm sorry, Aunty. I'm at Cynthia's house. I tried calling, but your line wasn't reachable."

Adonis, now awake, watched her with an amused smile.

"Cynthia?" Julianna repeated. "I thought you went out with your boyfriend?"

"No, Aunty, I'm at Cynthia's," Reana insisted, gripping the phone tightly. "I'll be home soon."

Before Julianna could question her further, she quickly ended the call.

Adonis chuckled. "Don't tell me I just made you lie."

"Of course, you did," she smirked.

"I'm sorry," he said, flashing an innocent glance.

"I have to go before she calls again," Reana said, sitting up.

Adonis ran a hand over her arm. "Did you enjoy last night? I hope I didn't hurt you."

Reana smiled. "No, baby. I enjoyed every moment. I told you I'd be ready the next time we spent the night together."

"Yeah, you did," he said hesitantly. "But... I didn't see any blood."

"You mean virgin blood?"

"Uh… yeah."

Reana smirked. "So I've been sleeping with other men, apparently?"

Adonis stiffened, his expression shifting.

She laughed. "Relax, I'm just messing with you. Not everyone bleeds."

"I thought I was hurting you. I almost stopped, but you…"

"…held you down," she finished for him. "I enjoyed it, Adonis."

His eyes softened. "I'm glad you did." He pulled her close and kissed her deeply.

Reana pulled away reluctantly. "Babe, we really need to go."

"Yeah, yeah, okay."

Minutes later, they stood outside the hotel gate, waiting for a taxi. Adonis waved one down, and they got in.

"Wait," Reana suddenly said. "I think I forgot my charger." She jumped out before Adonis could respond.

"Sorry, driver," Adonis said.

"No problem," the driver replied casually.

As he waited, Adonis noticed a red Venza pulling up in front of the restaurant next to the hotel. He watched as the doors opened. To his surprise, Felix—his friend—stepped out from the passenger seat, followed by an unfamiliar guy who emerged from the driver's seat.

They switched positions and soon the car was moving again.

Just then, Reana returned.

"Did you get it?" he asked.

"Yeah, sorry for the delay," she said, apologising to the driver.

Before the taxi could move, Adonis spoke up. "Driver, follow that red Venza."

Reana frowned. "Why?"

"There's someone inside that looks familiar. I'll explain later."

She gave him a pointed look. "I hope you're not getting into trouble again."

"Not at all," Adonis assured her. "Driver, please follow them slowly. I'll pay you anything. My girl will get off at the junction."

"Alright," the driver nodded.

As the Venza pulled away, the taxi followed closely. The car ahead moved faster, as if sensing they were being tailed. The taxi driver sped up to keep pace.

When they reached the street junction, Reana stepped out to catch another ride, but her mind was racing, wondering what Adonis was up to.

The taxi trailed the red Venza, mirroring its stops, turns, and changes in speed. As they drove, Adonis realised they had just passed the junction where he and his friends were arrested some time ago. A familiar unease crept over him.

The chase continued until the Venza came to a stop—just two meters away from the police station where they had been detained on the night of Osaretin's birthday. The same station where Damiete had gone missing.

Adonis' heart pounded. He motioned for the taxi driver to stop a meter behind the Venza, then quickly climbed to the front seat for a better view.

Felix stepped out of the Venza and walked straight towards the station.

"What the hell is he doing here?" Adonis muttered.

Confused and wary, Adonis pleaded with the driver.

"Please, just wait a little longer."

Meanwhile, when Reana got home, only her cousins were around. Aunty Julianna had already left for work.

"Welcome," Peter said. "We've been calling you since yesterday."

"I'm sorry," Reana replied, setting down her bag. "I was at Cynthia's house. I tried calling Mum, but her phone wasn't reachable."

Peter shook his head. "We almost went to the police station. We decided to wait till morning to see if you'd call or come home."

Reana let out a soft laugh.

"It's not funny," Joan cut in, visibly upset. "We were really scared. We even called your dad."

"Oh," Reana muttered. "So that's why he called me."

"You need to call Mum and let her know you're home," Peter added. "She's been checking in."

"Okay," she said and walked to her room.

Reana dialled her aunt's number, but there was no response.

She stepped into the shower, letting the warm water cascade over her skin. As the steam enveloped her, her mind drifted to the memories she had made with Adonis just hours ago. A shiver of pleasure ran through her… but then came the pang of regret.

Why do I feel like this?

A lump formed in her throat. Before she could stop herself, tears started rolling down her cheeks.

I love Adonis… but why do I always feel this emptiness after we get intimate?

The ache in her chest deepened.

"Why do I feel worse every time?" she muttered.

Frustrated, she grabbed her sponge and scrubbed her skin with force—so hard that it left her feeling raw and sore all over.

When she stepped out of the shower, she stood in front of the mirror, her reflection staring back at her, bruised and vulnerable. Her body bore the marks of her own frustration, but the deepest pain was invisible.

Then, a fresh wave of grief hit her. She sank to the floor, sobbing harder. Her sister's face flashed through her mind. A fresh wound reopened in her heart.

Meanwhile, at the station, the taxi driver was growing impatient.

"Oga, how long I go wait?" he muttered.

Adonis checked the time—nearly 30 minutes had passed.

"Please, just a little longer," he pleaded.

The driver huffed. "I no fit wait again, abeg."

Just as Adonis was about to tell him to drive off, Felix stepped out of the station.

"Wait."

Adonis watched as Felix walked back to the Venza, exchanged a few words with the guys inside, then turned around and re-entered the station.

Seconds later, a Hilux parked in front of the station roared to life. Felix climbed in. The vehicle sped off, with the Venza right behind it.

Adonis' instincts screamed at him. He had to follow.

"Driver, please, follow them," he urged.

But the driver had had enough. "Oga, I no dey do this

work with you again! I be taxi driver, no be action film I come act!"

Adonis exhaled sharply. "Fine. Just drop me at Johnson Street."

When Adonis got home, he dialled Nimi's number.

"What's up, Nimi?"

"I'm good, Adonis. Where have you been? We don't see you around anymore."

"I know, right? Well, you know I'm not a student like you."

"Come on now, how have you been?"

"I've been good," Adonis said. "Have you seen Felix lately?"

"Yes, I have. He's a big boy now," Nimi replied.

"Really? What do you mean 'big boy'? You know he's always been one."

"I know," Nimi chuckled, "but he's bigger now. He's driving a Venza these days."

"Wow. That's huge."

"Really huge."

"What does he do?" Adonis asked, his curiosity piqued.

"Come on now," Nimi said, lowering his voice. "What do you guys do these days?"

Adonis smirked. "Guys do a lot of things. I can only speak for myself."

"Well, we should all meet up. I need to eat all your money."

Nimi let out a loud laugh.

"You still keep in touch with him, right?" Adonis asked. "Call him and Osaretin. Any date, I'm down."

"Okay, I'll call him now and let you know what's up."

"Cool, Nimi. It's really nice hearing from you again. I'll be expecting your call."

"Me too," Nimi said. "I'll call you soon."

Adonis wasn't exactly surprised that Felix had a Venza or that he might be involved in internet fraud. What he didn't understand was why Felix was at the police station—the very place where Damiete had gone missing.

He sighed, pushing the thought aside for a moment, then suddenly remembered he hadn't checked in on Reana since she got home.

He picked up his phone and sent her a message.

Reana saw the notification flash across her screen but ignored it.

She wasn't sure what she was feeling—resentment towards Adonis or regret over what they had done. Either way, she needed time to process it.

The emotions swirling inside her didn't make sense. Why do I feel this way?

She put her phone down and curled up in bed, hoping sleep would silence her thoughts.

***

When it was almost noon, and Reana still hadn't replied or called, Adonis tried again.

This time, she picked up.

"Hello," she said, her voice neutral.

"I've been calling and texting you," Adonis said. "Where have you been?"

"I'm sorry, I was sleeping," she lied.

"Okay, I figured."

Reana kept her tone light, but inside, she was battling a

growing sense of resentment she couldn't explain. She should have been happy, but instead, she felt… empty.

She knew if she voiced her feelings, it would hurt Adonis. And she didn't want that—not until she could figure out what was wrong with her.

So she kept it to herself.

They chatted for a while, keeping the conversation casual. And when they hung up, Reana was left alone with her thoughts once again.

That evening, Adonis got a call from Nimi.

"Hello, the boys said they'd love to meet up by 7 PM Are you in?"

"Of course. What's the location?"

"I'll text it on WhatsApp."

"Alright. See you at 7."

"See you," Nimi responded.

As Adonis got ready, he sent a quick text to Reana.

ADONIS: Hi love, I'm meeting up with some friends this evening. Do you want to hang out?

Her reply came almost immediately.

REANA: No, I've already gotten in trouble with my aunt. I doubt she'll let me out again.

ADONIS: Okay, I understand.

There was a pause before another message popped up.

REANA: You still haven't told me who you were trailing in that Venza. You dropped me off so fast that day.

Adonis hesitated.

ADONIS: Oh, that? It wasn't who I thought it was.

He wanted to tell Reana the truth, but he couldn't. The threat from the senator and the police still lingered in his mind. Until he figured out what Felix was up to, he wasn't going to drag Reana into anything.

Seeing that Venza at the police station the day he was released and then seeing Felix in the same car going back there—it couldn't be a coincidence. Something was off, and he needed to find out what.

REANA: I guess I'll talk to you tomorrow?

ADONIS: Yes, but I might call before I go to bed. I love you.

REANA: Love you.

When Adonis arrived at Dotnova Hotel, he called Nimi, hoping they were already there. She directed him inside, and he got to the bar area, scanning the tables for his friends.

Then he spotted Felix, Osaretin, and Nimi sitting at a table with two other guys. One of them had a huge birthmark on his head, giving him a rough appearance.

"Adonis is in the building!" Osaretin called out.

Felix smirked. "This guy still won't stop wearing suit trousers everywhere."

Adonis grinned. "And you still won't stop rocking those crazy jeans."

"Okay, okay, you two never change," Nimi cut in, shaking his head.

Adonis turned to Osaretin. "You're looking chubby these days. Are you sure you're still in school?"

Osaretin laughed. "My guy, we have to enjoy life. But I'm not as chubby as Felix—look at him!"

Felix barely looked up from his phone, scrolling through something.

"Felix, what's up? You just got into school and forgot about your guys?" Adonis asked.

Felix raised his head slightly. "It's not like that, my guy. I've just been busy."

Nimi burst out laughing. "Busy making money!"

Felix smirked. "You can say that again."

Adonis leaned forward. "Since you're making all this money, show us the way now. We're your guys."

Osaretin nodded. "Exactly. Put us on."

Felix waved at the bartender for more drinks.

Adonis turned to the two unfamiliar guys at the table. "I greet you, my guys."

"We greet you, boss," they responded.

Adonis shifted his attention back to Felix. "So, what's the deal? Any hustle our 'little minds' can handle, we're in."

Felix leaned back, smirking. "This business is not for little minds."

The table erupted in laughter.

"Then make our minds bigger," Osaretin quipped.

"Abi," Adonis agreed. "You're doing well, though. I'm proud of you."

Felix nodded. "Thanks, bro."

Adonis sipped his drink. "So, what have you guys been up to?"

Osaretin groaned. "Just chilling at this point. I'm tired of that fucking school."

Adonis raised a brow. "You? I expected that from Felix."

Nimi chuckled. "Why Felix?"

Felix shrugged. "Bruh, I was tired even before I got into school."

Laughter filled the table.

"That's why I had to run away and cool off," Felix added.

Osaretin grinned. "Bro, that picture of you in Dubai was dope as fuck. You're really living life. Show us the way!"

Adonis nodded. "Yeah, stop dulling us."

Felix finally gave in. "Okay, guys. I maintain government websites and social media pages."

Osaretin's eyes widened. "That's huge!"

Adonis gave Felix a side-eye. "Link us up, na. What are friends for?"

"Abi o," Nimi agreed.

Felix exhaled. "I don't know if there are still slots available, but I'll let you guys know if I hear anything."

"Boss, we greet you!" Osaretin hyped, raising his glass.

Adonis laughed and shook Felix's hand. "Big man moves."

After much banter, Adonis leaned back and smirked. "But you know what I really want, Felix? Your Venza—to cruise around town."

Osaretin grinned. "Guy, it's like you read my mind."

Felix burst into laughter. "That's no biggie."

Adonis took a sip of his drink. "Funny thing is, I've been seeing your Venza around a lot. I think I even spotted it near that godforsaken police station once."

Felix's laughter faded. "Which station?"

"You know, the one where we were held when we all got arrested."

Felix frowned. "What would I be doing there? That wasn't me."

"Relax, I didn't say I saw you. I just saw a car that looked like yours," Adonis clarified.

Osaretin shrugged. "Maybe you're imagining things, bro."

Adonis shook his head. "Nah, for real. Maybe it was another brand, or maybe you just parked nearby to grab food or something. It was a bit far from the station, though."

Felix's tone hardened. "I'm telling you, I haven't been

anywhere near that area in a long while. What are you on about?"

Nimi raised her hands. "Guys, guys, we're here to chill, not argue."

Adonis exhaled. "I'm not arguing, just saying what I saw." He took another sip of his drink.

Felix didn't respond. The conversation shifted, and they kept chatting until Felix left. Not long after, the rest of them also headed home.

Later that night, Adonis' phone buzzed. It was Osaretin.

"Bro, what's up with you and Felix?"

Adonis frowned. "Nothing. Why asking?"

"It just felt like you were trying to rile him up."

"Me? Not at all, I was just teasing."

Osaretin hesitated. "But did you really see his car at that station?"

"Yes, I did," Adonis said.

"And you saw him too?"

"Yeah. He was entering the station."

Osaretin fell silent for a moment. "That's weird. Last time I asked him to go there with me to see if we could find out anything about Damiete, he flat-out refused. Even swore he'd never step foot there. And now you're saying you saw him?"

"I know what I saw," Adonis replied. "Well, he could have been there to see someone."

"Hmm. Okay, bro, we'll talk later."

"Alright, bro."

As Adonis hung up, a feeling gnawed at him. Felix was hiding something. Had he not lied about being there, it would have been a different story. But now Adonis had to learn the truth.

About a month later, Adonis ran into Felix at the mall. Felix pretended not to see him, but Adonis walked up to him anyway.

"My guy," Adonis called out.

"Ah! What's up, bro?" Felix responded, faking surprise.

"I'm good. You're still around?"

"Yeah, but I'm heading back to school this weekend. How are you and Reana?"

"We're good."

"I see. I actually saw you both strolling one time—I wanted to call out, but I wasn't quick enough. I was driving."

"Oh, okay."

Felix shifted his shopping bag. "I'm done here. I guess I'll see you around."

"Same here. Let me ride with you," Adonis said.

Felix hesitated but nodded. They left the mall together.

As they got into Felix's car, Adonis ran his hand over the dashboard. "This whip is more solid on the inside."

Felix gave a weak smile. "So, what have you been up to?" He asked.

"Nothing much. Just managing my workshop and I got a teaching job at a technical institute."

"That's nice. You're doing well for yourself, but you know you still need to go to school to become a professional architect. More people will take you seriously."

Adonis scoffed. "Guy, I already have plenty of people working with me. I'm good."

"If you say so," he said, dismissively.

As Felix merged onto the highway, a black Mercedes-Benz zoomed past, followed closely by a police Hilux truck, sirens blaring.

"These policemen are at it again," Adonis muttered, pulling out his phone to record.

Felix glanced at him. "What are you doing?"

"Capturing the moment."

"This stuff happens every day," Felix said flatly.

"Yeah, I know."

Suddenly, a boy tumbled out of the moving police Hilux, rolling onto the roadside.

"Jesus Christ! Did you see that?" Adonis exclaimed. "A boy just fell out of the police van! Do you see what these guys are doing?"

Gunshots rang out as the police continued chasing the Mercedes, leaving the boy behind.

By the time Felix and Adonis got to where he lay, a small crowd had already gathered.

"Let's check on him," Adonis suggested.

Felix barely glanced at the scene. "Why would I want to do that? I have somewhere to be. If you want to ask questions, I can drop you off."

Adonis turned to him, surprised at his indifference. Felix had barely reacted the whole time. His silence spoke volumes.

Without another word, Adonis stepped out of the car. Felix drove off.

Adonis watched as some passersby lifted the injured boy onto a motorbike, probably rushing him to a hospital. He approached a young man filming the scene on his phone. The guy was shouting angrily.

"This is what is happening to us now!" the man yelled.

"The police are chasing boys on the road, shooting in the air, all to extort money from the youth. Let the whole world see this!"

Adonis stepped closer. "Bro, what exactly happened?"

The guy turned to him, his voice rough with frustration. "These policemen have been harassing boys in this town—always trying to get money from us. You'd think they're out to arrest so-called yahoo boys, but instead, they just extort them and let them go, only to shake them down again another time. I got it all on video. I'm posting it on Twitter. Let the whole world see!"

It didn't take long for Adonis to piece things together. The boy who jumped out of the police van must have been arrested from that Mercedes and tried to escape. That was the only logical explanation.

Adonis flagged down a taxi and headed home.

On the way, he opened Twitter. The video was already circulating—with over a thousand views.

Nothing will happen, Adonis thought bitterly.

He stared at the recording he had taken on his phone, then, without hesitation, deleted it.

Something in his gut told him to because if the police searched his phone and found that video…

This time, he wouldn't make it out alive.

When he got home, Annetta ran to him. "My son, thank God you're home. I heard the police shot a boy dead today," she said as she stepped out of the kitchen into the sitting room where Adonis was.

Adonis looked up, startled. "Somebody died? Where did you hear that?"

"Everyone coming from town is saying it."

"Mum, no one died. A boy jumped out of a moving police Hilux, but he's alive. I saw him being taken away—

probably to the hospital."

Annetta frowned. "Why did he jump?"

"I don't know, but the police were chasing a car with young boys inside. He was likely one of them."

She shook her head. "I'm sure they're yahoo boys. The way they parade around town these days, their numbers just keep increasing."

Adonis sighed. "Mum, how do you know they're yahoo boys? Just because you see them in nice cars?"

"What kind of car was it?"

"A Benz."

Annetta scoffed. "Exactly. Isn't that what they drive? Let them arrest them."

Adonis leaned back, exasperated. "You really think arresting them changes anything? If these boys actually faced the law, why do their numbers keep growing? You guys aren't ready for that conversation."

Annetta shrugged. "I'm not a law enforcement agent. What's my own?"

"That's exactly the problem," Adonis shot back. "You older folks refuse to see the truth. Maybe those boys are into fraud, but how are they different from politicians and corrupt officers? Where are the jobs to keep young people from crime? What real efforts are being made to reduce fraud? These arrests are just about extorting money—most of them don't even make it to the station. Meanwhile, guess how many times I've been locked up for nothing? This country isn't serious."

Annetta sighed. "Ehn!! You're right, my son. But what can we do? All we can do is watch and pray, God will save us." She said, hesitantly.

Adonis let out a bitter laugh. "As usual waiting for heaven daddy to come down and save his grown children. That's why the country will never move forward—just sitting, watching, waiting for the next tragedy." Without another word, he walked to his room.

Annetta shook her head. "Na wa o!! I'm not even a police officer. What did I do?" she muttered to herself.

Later that evening, Adonis dialled Reana's number.

"Hello, Reana. Sorry I haven't called—I got delayed on the road. Can you imagine what I saw today?"

Her voice was quiet. "No, Adonis. I can't."

He frowned. "What's wrong? Why do you sound like that?"

A pause. Then, "I'm not feeling well. I had a miscarriage."

Adonis froze. "What?! I don't understand. Miscarriage? You were pregnant?"

"I was."

"I don't get it… We haven't done anything in a month. And last time, you took the pill, right?"

Another pause. "No, I didn't."

"What?!"

Her voice was flat. "Did you get it for me? Or was I supposed to get it myself? I didn't even know I was pregnant, Adonis."

He felt his chest tighten. "What happened?"

"This morning, I was about to sit when my cousin playfully pulled the stool away. I fell hard. Later, in the shower, I started bleeding. At first, I thought it was my period—it was overdue—but the bleeding was heavy, then it stopped suddenly and started again."

Adonis ran a hand over his face. "Oh my God, Reana. Where are you now? Are you still bleeding?"

"Yeah… slightly. I'm at home."

"We need to go to the hospital. I'm coming now."

"No, Adonis. I'll let you know if I need to go."

"What if something happens to you? Please, let's just meet at the hospital."

"I'm not bleeding that much. I'll call you back."

"Call me back?"

The line went dead.

Adonis redialed, but her number was switched off.

He stared at his phone, heart pounding.

Lately, she had been distant—ignoring his calls, making excuses to avoid meeting up.

And now this.

Something wasn't right.

The next morning, Adonis tried calling Reana on his way to his workshop, but she didn't pick up. When he arrived, he was surprised to see her standing at the entrance.

"Babe, I've been calling you."

"Please open the door. I won't stay long."

"Can we at least go to the hospital to make sure you're okay?"

"I'm fine." Reana glanced over his shoulder. "Why is a police Hilux parking outside?"

Adonis turned. A police vehicle had just pulled up, and a group of officers stepped out, huddling together as if trying to figure out where they were headed.

"Why are they coming to this area?" Reana asked.

"I have no idea."

The moment the officers started walking towards them, Adonis' instincts kicked in. He considered slipping out through the back, but before he could move, they were inside the workshop.

One of the officers grabbed him by the trousers. "So, you're the one posting videos of police officers, right?"

Adonis frowned. "I didn't post anything. I don't know what you're talking about."

"Shut up!" another officer barked. "You're going to tell us who you're working for."

A third officer eyed Reana. "This is your girl, right? Pick both of them!"

One of the men grabbed Reana's arm, but she yanked herself free. "You can't just arrest people without cause! Where's your warrant? Even if he posted a video, so what?!"

For a moment, the officers hesitated, caught off guard by her defiance.

Then, one of them snapped back into action. "Arrest them! They can explain themselves at the station!"

Adonis hadn't expected them to take Reana, but they did. As they were driven to the station, he spotted a familiar red Venza cruising past. He leaned towards Reana and whispered, "That's Felix's car."

She didn't respond.

At the station, the officers shoved him into a cell but locked Reana up in what used to be an old office, now filled with bad furniture.

She was almost in tears, yet fuming with anger. She felt the urge to tell the officers whose daughter she was, knowing full well they would realise their mistake in arresting her. But she hated associating herself with her father—she had always judged him for his actions.

Tension built in her chest. For a split second, she blamed herself for associating with someone who couldn't stay out of trouble. Realising this, she shook her head, pushing the thought away. She knew Adonis wasn't to blame—not in a country where trouble found you even when you tried to run from it.

She sighed, pacing to keep herself calm, cursing everything in her path. She checked her watch—she had been there for about forty-five minutes, and no one had come to open the door. Tired, she pulled out a chair and was about to sit when she heard Adonis scream.

Furious, she rushed to the door and banged on it. Within a minute, an officer appeared, angry. He grabbed her by the hair, making her cry out in pain. She fought back, but her strength was no match. He dragged her to a seat in the corridor.

Moments later, an officer escorted Adonis out. One of his eyes was swollen.

Seeing him, Reana rushed forward. "They did this to you?" She reached out to touch him, but he shrugged.

"I'm sorry I got you into this."

"It's fine. We'll be out of here soon," she said, glaring at the officer behind Adonis. Her face was a canvas of hate. She despised everything about the man—the way he held Adonis in cuffs like a criminal, the suffocating stench of the station, the wardens with their empty stares, moving about as if it were a marketplace. She hated everything.

An officer approached them. "Oya, make una follow me," he said, turning down the corridor.

She exchanged a look with Adonis before following, almost chuckling at the number of times the officer had patched his pants to keep them from falling apart. He had a strange way of walking, leaning forward as though he were about to tumble.

They reached a door, and he knocked. Without waiting for a response, he pushed it open and ushered them inside.

Sitting behind a desk was the DPO, flanked on both sides by officers. One was the light-skinned officer Adonis had seen at the counter and with the senator. The other had a scar on his forehead.

Adonis recognised him instantly. He had seen him before—sitting beside Felix at the bar.

It all made sense now. This was a setup.

The DPO's eyes narrowed when he saw Reana. "What is she doing here?" He turned to his men. "That's Oga's child. Why is she here?"

One of the officers hesitated. "Sir, she was with him when we found—"

"So why did you bring her here? Take her out—now!" The DPO's expression darkened. He turned to Reana. "We're sorry for the inconvenience, ma'am. You're free to go."

Reana folded her arms. "Why are you arresting him?"

"Madam, it's not your concern. You can leave."

Adonis met her gaze. "Please, just go."

She held his stare. "I'm getting you a lawyer." Then, turning to leave, she paused and gave the DPO a long stare.

The DPO leaned back in his chair and faced Adonis. "Where's the video from yesterday? The one you posted?" He noticed Reana still at the door and signalled an officer to escort her out.

Adonis exhaled. "I didn't post anything."

Then it hit him. The only person who knew he had recorded a video was Felix.

His mind raced, but there was no time to process the betrayal. He pulled out his phone and handed it over. "Check for yourself."

The DPO scoffed. "You think I'm stupid?"

"No, sir. I'm telling the truth. You can go through my social media, my last posts—anything. I wasn't the only one at the scene. I didn't post anything."

The DPO wasn't convinced. "Take him back to the cell."

An officer grabbed Adonis and dragged him away as he kept pleading.

Meanwhile, Reana had rushed to Adonis' parents' house, only to find no one home. She dialled Felix's number.

No response.

11

As usual, the industrial city of Port Harcourt buzzed with activity. The carbon-coated rooftops gave the skyline a rusty hue, and the symphony of car horns filled the air.

Under the historic Garrison Bridge, four young men and a woman stood firmly, holding up colourful placards with bold messages: **END POLICE BRUTALITY. STOP KILLING THE YOUTH. STOP EXTORTING THE YOUTHS.**

The day before, a video had surfaced online, showing police officers in pursuit of a Mercedes-Benz. The chase had ended with a young man injured—shot by the police. Outrage erupted across social media, fuelling anger among the youth, who swiftly organised a protest.

For over an hour, the small group stood their ground under the bridge, their signs high and their voices firm.

As more passersby took notice, curiosity turned into solidarity. People began joining in, snapping pictures and sharing them online. The protest was gaining momentum.

In their living room, Adonis' parents sat in anxious silence. His last message to Annetta had been brief:

I've been arrested. Don't come for me. I'll be out soon.

But it had been hours. Too many hours.

Mr Pere clenched his fists. "I can't just sit here and wait.

What if he never comes back and disappears like his friend?"

"Please don't say that," Annetta whispered, holding back tears. "He will come back."

A sudden knock on the door broke the tension. Annetta hurried to open it.

"Reana! How are you?"

"I'm fine, ma. But I need to talk to you."

"Come inside."

Reana stepped in and greeted Mr Pere.

"I'm fine, sir. But Adonis is in the police station."

They didn't look surprised.

"Yes, we know," Mr Pere said. "He texted us not to worry."

"He did?" Reana hesitated. "We have to get a lawyer. That station… it's the same station he was taken to the first time, where they claimed his friend escaped."

"What?!" Annetta gasped, her body trembling. "He never told us that." She collapsed to her knees, tears spilling down her face. "Why is this happening? Oh my God, this is the third time they've arrested him!"

Mr Pere placed a hand on her shoulder. "This is not the time to cry. We need to act."

"I think we need someone familiar with these policemen," Reana suggested.

Mr Pere's face hardened. "What exactly happened?"

Reana exhaled sharply. "They're questioning him about a video that was posted online. I don't know what video they mean, but the only one trending right now is a boy jumping out of a moving police vehicle while officers chased suspected Yahoo boys."

Annetta started pacing. "What has he gotten himself into this time?" she murmured. "He came home that day so upset. Oh God, please protect my son."

"I have to see our chairman," Mr Pere said, grabbing his keys.

After multiple failed attempts, Reana finally got through to Felix.

"Hello, Felix? Please, I need your help. Adonis has been arrested."

Felix sighed. "What did he do this time? He's always getting into trouble with the police."

He sounded like he already knew.

Reana's stomach tightened. "Why would you say that?" Her voice sharpened. "And how do you even know?" She knew Felix and Adonis hadn't been close since he left for school.

"What do you want me to do?" Felix asked, his tone indifferent.

"We need to get him out of there."

Behind her, Annetta suddenly stiffened. "Is that the boy called Felix?"

"Yes, ma."

"Drop the call!"

Reana hesitated. "Ma… why?"

Annetta's voice rose. "Drop it. What kind of friend talks like that? My son will be fine. We don't need his help."

Reana swallowed hard and ended the call. Slowly, she sat on the couch, pulling her knees together, fear tightening around her chest.

The room fell into a heavy silence as they waited for Mr Pere to return.

Afternoon faded into evening, yet there was still no sign of Mr Pere. Reana decided to head home.

Late into the night, the door creaked open. Annetta paused her prayers, expecting news—something, anything—

but instead, she found her husband stumbling inside, reeking of alcohol. He barely made it to the couch before collapsing onto it.

"So this is what you've been doing?" Annetta's voice was sharp with disbelief. "Your son is locked up, and while I've been here praying and waiting for answers, you went out drinking?"

Mr Pere scoffed, slurring his words. "Look here, I've done more than enough for your so-called son, but all he ever does is get into trouble. How do I know he's not a criminal?"

Annetta's eyes burned with fury. "You can think what you want, but I know my son is not a criminal!"

"Then why is he in jail? Leave me alone, I'm tired."

With that, he staggered out of the sitting room, leaving Annetta clutching her chest, her prayers turning into silent tears.

The next morning, Reana reached out to Rita Okogun, the activist who had organised the previous day's protest. The moment Rita learned about Adonis' arrest, she acted.

Within hours, the news spread across the internet—a young man detained for allegedly posting a video exposing police misconduct. Social media erupted, and it was announced that that day's protest would take place right in front of the police station where Adonis was being held.

Reana rushed to Adonis' house without informing her parents, but his family wasn't home. So she went straight to the police station, where the protest had already begun.

The air was thick with defiance. Hundreds of youths filled the street, chanting **"END POLICE BRUTALITY!"** and waving their placards. At the front of the crowd stood Rita

Okogun, gripping a megaphone, her voice steady as she rallied the protesters.

A woman stepped forward, gesturing for the megaphone. Rita hesitated for only a second before handing it over.

The woman climbed onto a stone pedestal and took a deep breath. "My brother went missing in this station. His name is Damiete."

The crowd fell silent.

"He was arrested with his friends. His friends came home. He never did. The DPO, Mr Chibuike Okafor, told my father that he escaped the night he was arrested, which his friends denied. That was the last we heard of my brother."

Gasps rippled through the protesters.

"Yes! Initially, I was told to bring a lawyer if I wanted to see my brother. Later on, the next day when I returned to the station, they told me he escaped the night he was arrested, which doesn't make sense. He is an innocent kid, just hanging out with his friend that day before he was snatched, and till today, we have not heard anything from my brother. They made him disappear and fed us lies." She turned to the station, now louder. "Mr Okafor, give me back my only sibling!"

Her voice cracked, and then she broke down in tears. "All I ask for is an explanation of my brother's whereabouts!"

The megaphone slipped from her hands as Rita rushed to comfort her.

Within minutes, Inspector Okafor's pictures flooded the internet. Activists and influencers placed bounties on his whereabouts.

Then, another protester stepped forward. "My brother was also killed in this station! His body was never found!"

The rage in the crowd swelled, turning into a storm.

A voice rose from the midst of the protesters—"We want to see why people are dying in this station, or we will burn it to the ground!"

The tension was about to snap when a female police officer emerged from the station. She raised her hands, trying to calm the crowd, but they refused to listen.

Reana pushed through the bodies, stepping forward. "Please, let's hear what she has to say!"

The officer nodded gratefully before addressing them. "My name is DPO Florence Nwosu. I understand your pain. I hear your cries. And I promise to investigate these accusations—but I need time. Please, if you have complaints, we will address them critically."

The murmurs of disagreement grew louder. By now, the crowd had nearly tripled.

Reana stepped forward again. "Since when did the police start arresting people in their homes and workplaces for posting videos online? Is it because the video exposed police misconduct?"

DPO Nwosu furrowed her brows. "What do you mean?"

Reana's voice trembled, but she spoke anyway. "My friend, Adonis, and I were arrested at his workshop for no reason. When we got to the station, they told me I wasn't the one they wanted, so they let me go. But before I left, I heard them accuse Adonis of posting a negative video about the police—even though he didn't."

The DPO inhaled deeply. "I don't know about that, but I will look into it. What's his name?"

"Adonis Pere."

She turned to one of the officers. "Go check on the boy."

The crowd erupted into chants again.

Reana stepped aside and quickly dialled Annetta. "Please don't come to the station. There's a protest going on here."

But Annetta's voice came through, calm but firm. "I'm already here. Where are you?"

Reana's head shot up. She turned and saw them—Annetta, Mr Pere, and their street chairman, Mr Donald, making their way through the crowd.

"I gave Adonis' name to the DPO," Reana told them. "She promised to look into it."

Annetta frowned. "Which DPO? The man who killed Adonis' friend?"

"No," Reana said quickly. "It's a woman. I think she's new."

They stepped aside from the restless crowd, waiting. Hoping.

By 7 PM, there was still no word from the DPO. The crowd had dwindled earlier, but as the night stretched on, it began to swell again. Two women had started distributing food and drinks, drawing more people back to the protest.

Reana urged Adonis' parents to go home—it was getting late—but they refused.

At around 7:30 PM, the DPO finally emerged. The moment she laid eyes on Annetta and Mr Pere, recognition flickered in her gaze. She remembered them from years ago—at the hospital where her friend, Adonis' biological mother, Karisha, had given birth. But they didn't recognise her.

"These are Adonis' parents," Reana introduced them.

The DPO greeted them warmly. "I assure you, I'm doing everything I can to get Adonis out."

"Then why is it taking so long?" Annetta demanded.

"I promise you, he will be released. But for now, I need you to go home."

"No," Annetta said firmly. "I'm not going anywhere until I see my son."

The crowd, noticing the conversation, began gathering again.

"Please," the DPO urged, lowering her voice. "Go home. Your son will be released in the morning—I give you my word. We're about to lock up for the night, and I can't predict what might happen."

"What do you mean?" Mr Donald asked suspiciously.

"Just trust me. Go home." The DPO's urgency was unmistakable. Then, without another word, she turned and hurried back inside the station.

What she didn't tell them was that Adonis had already been transferred to another location.

Reana tried to persuade Annetta and Mr Pere to leave.

"Please, my dear," Annetta pleaded. "Let's all go. I can't leave you here—your parents will be worried."

"Don't worry," Reana reassured her. "I'm right behind you. We're going in opposite directions anyway."

Reluctantly, Annetta and Mr Pere left.

Mr Donald, however, remained, soon swallowed by the sea of protesters.

By 9 PM, the police station was completely shut down. The lights—both inside and on the street—were switched off. The air was thick with tension.

Then came the sound of approaching engines.

Four vans, packed with armed police officers, rolled in from both ends of the street. The crowd erupted into chants:

"END POLICE BRUTALITY!"

"STOP KILLING THE YOUTH!"

Reana's pulse quickened. She turned to escape, but the road was blocked. The police officers climbed out, brandishing their guns, forming a tight line in front of the protesters.

Then, one of the vans reversed, momentarily opening a path. A few protesters rushed towards the gap—only for gunfire to split the night.

The chaos was instant.

Reana dropped to the ground, pressing herself flat against the asphalt. Others did the same, while some panicked and ran—only to collapse as bullets tore through them.

She fumbled for her phone, her fingers trembling. Live.

She needed to go on Instagram Live.

"They are shooting at us," she whispered, her breath ragged. "We came here to protest peacefully against police brutality, and they're killing us."

Her screen illuminated the horror—people screaming, bodies falling. A protester beside her jerked violently before going still. Blood pooled beneath him.

More shots. More bodies.

Reana kept streaming, her voice breaking.

Then her phone went off. She knew she would have to remain this way, with no means to contact anyone since her battery was flat.

Silence followed the last gunshot, eerie and unnatural. From her hiding place, Reana watched as the officers methodically moved through the carnage, dragging bodies into their vans. They picked up shell casings, erasing traces of the massacre.

When they finally left, those who had survived began to emerge, voices rising in grief and rage. The wailing of sirens filled the air as ambulances arrived.

Reana stood frozen, unable to process what she had just witnessed.

She stepped forward, her vision swimming. A boy was being lifted onto a stretcher—his stomach split open, intestines spilling out.

A metallic tang filled her nostrils. Blood. Gunpowder.

Her stomach lurched. She bent over and vomited.

This wasn't a protest anymore. It was a massacre.

Adonis knew he was in a different cell the moment the light flickered on. He had been blindfolded when they moved him, but now, as he took in his surroundings, it was clear this wasn't an ordinary holding cell. There were no windows—at least, none that were visible. The room felt more like a basement than a detention centre.

Then, he spotted it. A window well, covered with wooden planks. Hope sparked inside him. Carefully, he pushed against the iron gate blocking the well. To his surprise, it gave way with little resistance.

Without hesitation, he squeezed himself into the narrow space, feeling the cold walls press against his skin. It wasn't an escape route—at least, not to the outside world. Instead, the tunnel led to another room.

As he reached the end, he heard voices. Pressing his ear against the surface above, he froze.

It was Felix.

"If he stays here, many things will be revealed. It's best we release him," Felix said, his voice urgent. "I can't sacrifice another friend."

Another voice responded, cold and dismissive. "Your friend is a fool. He should be dead already. If that's why you're here, you need to leave. I'll send you your share when everything is sold. Apart from tying up a loose end, this is a lot of money we're talking about."

Adonis' stomach clenched. He knew that voice. The senator.

Realisation crashed into him.

He was in the underground warehouse—the very one

he had designed for the senator. Except, the senator hadn't followed all his blueprints.

His pulse pounded in his ears as the pieces fell into place. Felix. It was him all along.

Memories flooded his mind.

Felix slipping his hand into Damiete's pocket the night of their arrest—something Adonis hadn't thought much of at the time.

Felix insisting on taking a different route that night.

His sudden disappearance after being released.

Adonis' second arrest after his Twitter post.

The threatening message from an anonymous account.

The police showing up at his home.

The red Venza at the station—the one Felix had denied ever being in.

And then, his third arrest. The video.

Only Felix knew about that video.

Adonis' breath came in sharp bursts. Was it all just about money? Or was Felix involved in something even darker? Human trafficking? Organ trade?

He didn't want to believe it. But deep down, he already knew the answer.

He pushed the thought aside. He needed to get out first. Everything else would have to wait.

For some days, the police station remained locked.

At dawn, on the seventh day, Adonis' parents and Reana arrived, determined to confront the DPO. They had come very early, hoping to speak with her before she entered the station.

But no one was allowed in.

Two hours passed. When the DPO finally arrived, they

rushed towards her, only to be blocked by officers.

"Stand down," she ordered, stepping towards them.

Annetta wasted no time. "Where is my son?" she demanded, her voice cracking with emotion.

The DPO exhaled. "I have information on his whereabouts, and I'm doing everything I can to get him out. Please, have a little patience."

"Patience?" Annetta's voice rose. "You promised he would be released, but my son is still missing. You people murdered protesters right in front of this station—tell me, is my son dead or alive?"

Mr Pere's voice was quieter but no less desperate. "Please. Tell us the truth."

The DPO straightened. "Madam, we did not kill anyone."

Reana's head snapped up. "What?" she hissed. "I saw it. I streamed it. The whole world saw it."

The DPO met her gaze, unflinching. "Adonis is alive, and I'll do everything I can to get him out. But like I said—we did not kill anyone."

Reana stepped forward, fury tightening her features. "Then who did?" she shot back. "It happened right here, outside your station!"

People across the street had started watching the exchange. The DPO glanced around before lowering her voice.

"Forces beyond our control," she murmured before turning on her heel and walking briskly into the station.

Annetta moved to follow, but the officers raised their guns.

"Go ahead," Reana spat. "Shoot us. That's what you do best, isn't it? Kill innocent people. Shoot us!" She stepped forward, daring them.

Annetta grabbed her arm, pulling her back.

They watched in silence as the officers filed into the station and shut the gates behind them.

Fifteen minutes later, a police officer emerged. He walked up to Annetta and spoke in a low tone.

"The DPO has instructed me to let you in."

Annetta hesitated, then nodded.

As she disappeared into the station, Reana and Mr Pere remained outside, waiting.

"Please, sit down," the DPO said, gesturing to a chair.

Annetta obeyed, her movements slow and weary. Her eyes, red and swollen, brimmed with unshed tears. She looked thinner than she was some days ago.

"You don't seem to remember me," the DPO continued.

Annetta blinked in confusion.

"I'm Mrs Elizabeth Chijioke. I was a friend of your late sister, Karisha."

Annetta frowned, searching her memory. "I don't remember you."

"I was at the hospital the day she died."

Annetta dropped her gaze and sighed, the weight of old grief settling over her.

"The boy you're looking for..." Elizabeth paused. "He's her son, isn't he?"

Annetta lifted her head. "Yes, he is."

Elizabeth exhaled deeply. "His name is Adonis?"

"Yes."

"I know who can get him out."

Annetta leaned forward, desperate. "Who?"

"His father."

Annetta froze. "I don't know his father. My sister never told me."

"She wouldn't have," Elizabeth said quietly. "Your sister

never wanted anything to do with the man who raped her. She only told me, and she made me swear never to tell anyone. When she died, I kept that promise. There was no reason to bring it up."

Annetta's heart pounded. "So why are you telling me now?"

Elizabeth's expression darkened. "Because his father is involved in this case. And that girl outside—she's his daughter."

Annetta's breath caught. Her pulse hammered in her ears. "What did you just say?"

"My men informed me that Reana… is Aza Briggs' child."

Annetta's hands trembled. "Reana? That wicked man's daughter?" She wanted to scream but held it in. There was no time to dwell on the implications. A bigger problem loomed.

"We need her to call her father and demand Adonis' release," Elizabeth said urgently. "You have to convince her. I'll do what I can from this end, but no one can know I'm involved."

"Thank you," Annetta murmured, rising from her seat. She moved quickly towards the door.

"We need to hurry," Elizabeth called after her. "While Adonis is still alive."

"Let's go," Annetta said firmly as she stepped outside, her eyes locking onto Reana and Mr Pere.

"Go where? What did they say?" Mr Pere asked, worry etched across his face.

"What's happening?" Reana pressed.

"Reana, come with me," Annetta said. "I'll explain everything when we get home."

Inside the house, Annetta turned to Reana.

"I have to tell you something."

Reana nodded. "Okay, Ma."

Annetta hesitated for a moment before asking, "Is Aza Briggs your father?"

Reana's breath caught. Her body stiffened. She rarely spoke about her father, even to Adonis.

"Yes," she admitted cautiously.

Annetta's expression tightened. "He's involved in Adonis' case."

Reana stared at her, waiting for more, but Annetta fell silent.

Reana's mind raced. She wasn't surprised—she had long suspected her father was involved in shady dealings. But hearing it out loud, from Annetta of all people, made it real.

Without a word, she turned and walked out.

She didn't go straight home. Instead, she went to her aunt's house.

As she entered, her aunt sat in the living room, watching her with sharp eyes.

"Reana!" she called as the younger woman walked past without greeting. "Reana, what's going on? You barely stay home. You refuse to go back to school. Everywhere is tense outside, and this is not the time to be wandering around."

"Aunty, please, not now," Reana muttered.

Her aunt wasn't having it. "Reana, tell me what's wrong."

"Nothing!" Reana snapped.

Her aunt blocked her path. "Then why have you been acting like this? When you do come home, you barely say a word. I saw the livestream the other night—I knew you were there."

Reana stiffened, her eyes widening in shock.

Her aunt gave her a knowing look. "At first, I didn't

realize it was you who posted it. But days later, I saw another post from that account, and I checked the page. I recognized our garden. The dogs. But no pictures of you. That's when I knew it had to be you—I know Joan and Peter's accounts. I thought about confronting you, but you've been running in and out of this house like a ghost."

Reana clenched her jaw, gripping the strap of her bag.

"Listen to me," her aunt continued, her voice softer now. "You know how they arrest young people these days over social media posts. Be careful. Don't think your father can always protect you."

Reana's eyes darkened with anger. "Why do you think I need his protection?"

Without waiting for an answer, she stormed out, ignoring her aunt's calls behind her.

Reana arrived at her family compound and was taken aback by how much had changed—but not for the better.

The once lush, evergreen flowers that lined the perimeter were now dry and withering.

Though the building had a fresh coat of paint, the entire place felt lifeless, weighed down by an unsettling stillness. The silence was thick, graveyard-like.

Several cars sat in the parking lot, their surfaces layered with dust.

On the front porch, a group of men loitered, their presence unmistakably that of bodyguards.

Reana ignored them and walked past, knowing her father would be inside—he had nowhere else to go, bound as he was to a wheelchair.

Inside, she found Becky, her father's wife, sitting at the dining table. Draped in an extravagant gown fit for a red carpet, she was flawless, every strand of hair in place. She turned, surprised to see Reana.

Reana frowned. *Was there a celebration? If so, she needed to leave—immediately.* She had no intention of sitting through any of their ridiculous theatrics.

"Good afternoon. May I come in?"

Becky barely glanced up. "You already have. This is your father's house; you don't need to ask. You're welcome anytime." Her voice was smooth, practiced, like an actress in a role she played too often.

Reana eyed her with disdain. The woman reeked of pretence.

"Where is my father?"

"In his room."

Reana turned and walked straight into her father's bedroom, the door already ajar.

Aza was on a call. When he saw her, his hand trembled slightly as he ended it.

"Catherine!" His voice was hoarse, uneven, as if the words pained him.

Reana stiffened. "My name is Reana."

She was astonished that, even in his weakened state, confined to a wheelchair, his speech impaired, he still barked out commands as though the world owed him obedience.

Aza studied her. She had grown beautiful—just like her mother. The pictures he had seen of her over the years hadn't lied.

Reana, however, saw none of the admiration in his gaze. All she saw was a frail man, more bones than flesh, his hands and feet twitching involuntarily.

"How are you, Catherine?"

"I didn't come here for pleasantries. Why did you arrest my friend?"

Aza raised a brow. "And which friend is so important that you forget to greet your father?"

Reana exhaled sharply. "Good afternoon."

He stared at her, unsatisfied.

She rolled her eyes. "Good afternoon, sir."

Aza finally spoke. "Now, who is this friend?"

"His name is Adonis."

A flicker of something crossed Aza's face, but it disappeared as quickly as it came. "I don't know anything about that name."

"Please," Reana pressed, her tone urgent. "If you know who has him, tell them to let him go. He's my friend. I don't want him to die."

"Where is he being held?"

"Mile 12 Police Station."

Aza scoffed. "I hope he wasn't part of that stupid protest."

Reana's stomach twisted at his words. *Did he have anything to do with murders? With the disappearances?* But she pushed the thought aside—Adonis came first. She had to get him out before confronting her father.

Aza studied her for a long moment, then said, "Wait outside."

She turned without another word.

Minutes later, he called her back in. "He will be released tomorrow."

Reana let out a breath she didn't realise she'd been holding. "Okay. Thank you."

She was about to leave when Aza spoke again. "How is your mother?"

She barely restrained a scoff. "Maybe you should call her. Instead," she mumbled. "She's fine."

"And you? How is school?"

Reana's patience snapped. "I didn't come here for small

talk," she said curtly and left, not sparing him another glance.

She walked past Becky, who was still seated at the dining table, untouched by the tension that had filled the air moments ago.

Once outside, sorrow wrapped around Reana like a thick cloak.

Her childhood played in the back of her mind—the blurred, questionable memories, the screams behind closed doors, the desperate cries for help. Pain coursed through her veins, the echoes of her past seeping into the present.

She couldn't bear to face Adonis' mother. Instead, she made the call, relaying the information as quickly as possible. It was easier this way.

By the time she got home, she was emotionally drained.

Adonis was taken back to the police station, blindfolded, his hands tied behind his back like a common criminal— or worse, a kidnapped man. His feet stumbled over uneven ground as unseen hands shoved him forward.

Through the back entrance, they led him, rough hands pushing him into a dimly lit cell. The door slammed shut.

Minutes later, the heavy creak of iron hinges echoed through the space. The blindfold was yanked off.

"Excuse us," a voice commanded.

The officer stepped aside, revealing a woman in uniform. The DPO.

"I'm very sorry for all you've been through these past few days," she said gently, crouching to his level.

Adonis kept his head down, saying nothing.

"You've grown so much. I can't believe I once held you when you were just a baby."

His gaze snapped up, eyes narrowing.

She smiled sadly. "Yes, Adonis. I was there when you were

born. I was your mother's friend. You can ask me anything."

Confusion flickered across his face. He had never met anyone who claimed to know his biological mother. Did it even matter now? Yet, despite himself, he had questions—questions he wasn't sure he wanted the answers to.

"Do you know who my father is?"

The DPO sighed, hesitating. "Your father is Aza Kio Briggs."

Adonis let out a sharp breath. "Which Aza?"

"The one you know."

He lowered his gaze. "Which Aza do I know?"

But deep down, he already knew.

Aza. The notorious godfather of Port Harcourt. Reana's father.

A spear of disbelief tore through him.

Reana had never spoken much about her father, always brushing off any questions. He had known her last name, of course, had connected the dots—but the truth had never fully settled in his mind.

She always said she had disowned her father. He never took her seriously.

But now?

"Aza cannot be my father," he whispered.

The DPO held his gaze. "Yes, he is. Your mother told me everything."

His mind reeled. "How? Were they… married? Dating?"

The DPO went silent. She knew Aza might not like to know how he came about.

Adonis could feel the weight of an unsaid truth hanging in the air.

"Please tell me," he pressed. "Did I come out of love… or just a mistake?"

The DPO stood. "Why does it matter?"

"You told me to ask anything," he shot back.

She exhaled deeply before answering.

"He raped your mother."

The words felt like a blade to his chest.

Adonis clenched his jaw, fighting against the rising tide of emotion. A storm raged inside him—pain, rage, disgust. His breath came out in shallow, uneven gasps.

Then the memories of Reana began to flux in. The way their connection had always felt strange. Unreal, he understood why.

"Let's go," the DPO said softly. "You're free."

But Adonis couldn't move. His feet were cemented to the ground, his body frozen.

How could he face Reana?

The DPO touched his arm. "It's okay. I'm glad your aunt has been taking good care of you." She smiled faintly. "What a coincidence—you've been friends with your sister all this time."

Sister.

The word sliced through him, deeper than any wound.

"She's your friend, right?"

Adonis didn't answer. But his face told the truth.

The DPO sighed. "You didn't know. The universe knows you were both innocent."

He swallowed hard, forcing his legs to move. Step by step, he walked out of the cell.

At the front desk, they handed him his belongings.

He was free but the weight in his chest told him otherwise.

Annetta cried out in joy when she saw him, rushing to embrace him. But as her arms wrapped around Adonis, she shivered—he was cold to the touch. His face was a shadow of itself, his once-bright eyes now dull, red, and swollen. His body, once strong, had become lean, almost fragile.

She guided him inside while neighbours gathered, celebrating his return.

The moment he stepped into the house, he spoke, his voice flat.

"Reana is my sister."

Annetta stilled. "It's not your fault. None of this is your fault."

"Did you know?"

"No. Your mother never told me anything about your biological father. She was always secretive about her past, but… in this case, I understand why. If she were alive, I know she would have told you herself."

"Does she know?"

"Who? Reana? No, she doesn't. I haven't said anything to her."

"How did you find out?"

"The same way you did. The DPO. She was your mother's friend."

Adonis exhaled sharply, rubbing his face. "I'm not ready to tell her."

Annetta nodded. "That's okay."

"Does Daddy know?"

"Yes. He does."

Adonis clenched his jaw. "We need to leave this town. I can't stay here anymore."

Annetta reached for his hand. "I know. Your dad and I have already decided—we're moving." She hesitated. "But I need to call Reana and tell her you're home."

"No, Mum. Please don't."

"She deserves to know. She's the reason you were released."

Adonis frowned. "What do you mean?"

"Her father was involved in your arrest. The DPO told us to inform her, so she could speak to him about letting you go… unharmed."

Everything felt like a dream. A terrible, twisted dream. Nothing made sense anymore.

Annetta picked up the phone and dialled.

"Reana, Adonis is home."

"Okay."

The line went dead.

Annetta stared at the phone, stunned.

The next morning, Reana's phone rang.

It was her mother. It had been a while since they last spoke. At first, she hesitated to pick up, but after the second buzz, she answered. Her mother revealed that her father had just died.

Reana was shocked—she had seen him only two days ago.

Cold swept over her, yet sweat trickled down her skin.

Her hatred for him had been vast, immeasurable. But now, it shifted into something she never thought she'd feel— sadness, pity, and regret.

She had always imagined a day would come when he would face her and apologise. Tell her he loved her.

She had hoped he would explain everything—that there was a reason for it all, that he wasn't the monster people whispered about. She had wanted him to deny the killings, to beg for forgiveness, to repent.

Now, that day would never come. He was already gone, and the questions she had carried for years would remain unanswered.

"Ladies and gentlemen, welcome to this special broadcast as we commemorate the life and legacy of the esteemed Aza Kio Briggs."

Reana sat motionless, watching the TV as the news anchor spoke with reverence.

"Today, we honour a man whose contributions to our society have left an indelible mark. Aza Kio Briggs was not just a politician; he was a visionary, a man who understood the pulse of the people and dedicated his life to their service.

Throughout his career, Briggs was a beacon of hope to many. His generosity knew no bounds, as he provided financial support to those in need, ensuring that no one was left behind.

His commitment to community development saw the establishment of schools, clinics, and infrastructure that continue to serve us to this day. These developments, though modest, were significant stepping stones towards progress in our community.

It is important to remember that Briggs' legacy is not merely about the tangible contributions he made but about the spirit of giving and unity that he fostered. He believed in uplifting the poor and giving a voice to the voiceless.

His commemoration is a reminder of these values, encouraging us to carry forward his mission of service and unity. As we celebrate his life, let us reflect on the good he brought into our world and strive to embody the principles he championed.

Aza Kio Briggs may no longer be with us, but his spirit lives on through the positive changes he inspired. Let us honour his memory by continuing to build a society based on compassion, integrity, and progress."

Reana's fingers curled into fists. "Lies."

If she hadn't known the truth, she might have believed every word of it.

For her, Aza Kio Briggs wasn't done with living—even in death. She swore that her father was too evil to leave this world like a saint.

With that, she made up her mind. She wouldn't be silent. If she had to be the one to expose his wrongdoing, so be it. She would do it not just to reveal the truth and expose the dark side of political leaders, but also as an effort to make reparation for her father's sins.

THE END

ACKNOWLEDGEMENTS

No book is ever written in isolation, and *Impunity* is no exception. This story was shaped by the realities around me, the voices that shared their truths, and the unwavering support of those who believed in its message.

First and foremost, I want to thank Sylvester Osakpolor for his invaluable contributions. Your insights, encouragement, and support played a crucial role in bringing this book to life. Your belief in this project gave me the strength to push forward, even when the weight of the story felt overwhelming.

To my family and friends, who have always stood by me, offering their love, patience, and understanding—I am deeply grateful. Your support fuels my passion for storytelling.

To my readers, who dare to confront the harsh realities of our world through literature—this book is for you. May it provoke thought, spark conversation, and inspire change. And above all, I thank God for the gift of creativity and the strength to tell stories that matter.

To Bayo Moses, Pius Daniel, and Jedidiah and the rest of the Madda Book Media team for their publishing expertise and managing my book project.

ABOUT THE AUTHOR

Faith Osemudiamen Ebhodaghe, who also writes under the pen name Faith Osemudiamen, Ivhade F.E.O, is a fiction writer from Edo State, Nigeria. Growing up in an extended family within a low-class neighborhood, she experienced a vivid and challenging childhood before moving to another town with her mother and sister. Osemudiamen pursued a first degree in Medical Laboratory Science and later honed her literary skills through short courses in creative writing and psychology.

In 2019, Osemudiamen penned her first book, *Dazed*, marking the beginning of her writing journey. Her literary interests span thriller, politics, religion, and romance genres. Drawing inspiration from real-life encounters, Osemudiamen is influenced by renowned authors such as Chimamanda Adichie and Dan Brown. Her writing delves into profound themes like good and evil, bravery, hardship, abuse, and religion.

Apart from writing, Osemudiamen has a passion for drawing and painting, particularly figurative drawing. She is currently engrossed in crafting a fiction story that explores the intriguing concept of astral projections and the dark side of beauty and femininity. Connect with her on Twitter/Instagram @ faithose_iv to stay updated on her latest works and musings.

www.ingramcontent.com/pod-product-compliance
Lightning Source LLC
Chambersburg PA
CBHW020317160726
47992CB00004B/1583